'TIL DEATH DO US PART

JEPH LOEB
STUART IMMONEN
JOE KELLY
MARK SCHULTZ
J.M. DeMATTEIS
JAY FAERBER
Writers

ED McGUINNESS
YANICK PAQUETTE
STUART IMMONEN
PABLO RAIMONDI
KANO
DOUG MAHNKE
Pencillers

CAM SMITH
RICH FABER
JOSÉ MARZÁN, JR.
SEAN PARSONS
JOE RUBINSTEIN
TOM NGUYEN
MARLO ALQUIZA
Inkers

TANYA & RICHARD HORIE
GLENN WHITMORE
WILDSTORM FX
Colorists

RICHARD STARKINGS & COMICRAFT
BILL OAKLEY
KEN LOPEZ
JOHN COSTANZA
Letterers

SUPERMAN created by JERRY SIEGEL & JOE SHUSTER

'TIL DEATH DO US PART

DC COMICS

SUPERMAN: 'TIL DEATH DO US PART

Published by DC Comics.

Originally published in single magazine form as SUPERMAN 155, THE ADVENTURES OF SUPERMAN 577, SUPERMAN: THE MAN OF STEEL 99, ACTION COMICS 764, SUPERMAN 156, THE ADVENTURES OF SUPERMAN 578, SUPERMAN: THE MAN OF STEEL 100, ACTION COMICS 765, SUPERMAN 157.

DC Comics, 1700 Broadway, New York, NY 10019
A division of Warner Bros. - An AOL Time Warner Company
Printed in Canada. First Printing.
ISBN: 1-56389-862-4
Cover illustration by Doug Mahnke & Tom Nguyen.
Cover color by Tanya & Richard Horie.

Sometimes, the simple truths, the ones that are staring at you as big as a barn door, are the hardest ones to see.
LADIES AND GENTLEMEN OF METROPOLIS AND THE WORLD, SUPERMAN AND I STAND HERE NOW, AS A SYMBOL OF UNITY --
-- A SYMBOL OF FRIENDSHIP--
-- A SYMBOL OF THE FUTURE FOR THE CITY THAT STANDS FOR ALL OF THOSE THINGS.
TRY NOT TO LAY IT ON SO THICK, LUTHOR.
JIM, SEE IF YOU CAN GET A SHOT WHERE LUTHOR'S EGO ISN'T PUSHING SUPERMAN OUT OF THE FRAME.

LEXCORP
I got to thinking about Ben Hubbard the other day. He bought Caleb Stone's farm up the way after Caleb died two winters ago.
SINCE NEW YEAR'S DAY, ALL EYES HAVE BEEN ON METROPOLIS.
OUR CITY WHICH ALWAYS HAS STOOD FOR ACHIEVING THE IMPOSSIBLE HAS NOW DONE THE IMPOSSIBLE.
IN LESS THAN MONTH, A WEEK, A DAY, IT HAS BLOSSOMED LIKE A BUTTERFLY OUT OF A COCOON AND STANDS NOW AS TRULY--
--"THE CITY OF TOMORROW!"
BUT, WE KNOW WHAT SOME OF YOU, JUST A FEW, ARE THINKING.
WITH ALL THIS NEW-"FANGLED" TECHNOLOGY IS OUR CITY SAFE?
AND SUPERMAN AND LEX LUTHOR ARE HERE TO GIVE YOU A SOLID, RESOUNDING--
YES.
I -- I AGREED TO BE HERE THIS MORNING NOT BECAUSE I WANTED TO BE A SYMBOL OF ANYTHING --
-- BUT BECAUSE OF THE RESPECT I HAVE FOR THE HARD-WORKING PEOPLE OF THIS CITY.
I'VE DONE WHAT I CAN, WITH PEOPLE WHO I TRUST, TO INVESTIGATE THE BUILDINGS, THE STREETS, AND THE PUBLIC AREAS FOR ANY POSSIBLE DANGERS.
AND, AT LEAST, FOR NOW, I'M SATISFIED THAT METROPOLIS IS A PLACE WORTH HOLDING ONTO.
BUT I STRONGLY ENCOURAGE EACH OF YOU TO COME TO YOUR OWN CONCLUSIONS.
ASK QUESTIONS, WRITE OR E-MAIL--
-- I DON'T THINK I COULD HAVE SAID IT BETTER MYSELF.
I'M SURE WE'D ALL LIKE TO HEAR MORE FROM SUPERMAN, BUT, AS WE KNOW --
-- FOR EVERY TWENTY GOOD CITIZENS, THERE ARE A FEW BAD APPLES WHO WOULD SPOIL IT FOR ALL OF US --
AND I'D GLADLY PUT YOU AT THE TOP OF THAT LIST, LUTHOR.
ISN'T THAT A CAT I HEAR CRYING UP SOME TREE?
-- SO LET'S GIVE HIM A BIG METROPOLIS CHEER AND HAVE SUPERMAN GET BACK TO PATROLLING OUR SKYWAYS AND BYWAYS!
NOW, THEN. I'LL BE HAPPY TO ANSWER ANY AND ALL OF YOUR QUESTIONS.

SIGH
IT'S YOUR SHOW, LUTHOR.
FOR TODAY.
Old Ben -- that's what we call him even though he can't be more than a year or two older than me -- likes to take to bragging about his boy.
Tom Hubbard, the son, went off to Harvard and Europe and all sorts of places before he settled somewhere out west like Los Angeles.
He's a lawyer or a doctor or both, I can't really remember. And while I'm not about to go beating my own chest about whose son has done what --
-- I don't know many that can stand side by side with my Clark.

...or even that punchy prose style that's made him the most sought-after reporter in Metropolis or anywhere for that matter...

HELLO? MA? PA?

IN THE *DINING ROOM*, CLARK -- AND WE'VE GOT *COMPANY!*

WISK

No, the plain, simple truth is that Ben Hubbard's boy can get appointed to the Supreme Court for all I care...

... he doesn't come home to visit his folks anymore. Too busy to write. Too busy to pick up the phone.

I can never appreciate enough that Clark still takes the time to drop by --

-- even when he's not expected.
The PRIVATE LIFE of CLARK KENT
JEPH LOEB Writes
ED McGUINNESS Pencils
CAM SMITH Inks
TANYA & RICHARD HORIE Colors
RICHARD STARKINGS Letters
MAUREEN McTIGUE Associates
EDDIE BERGANZA Edits
SUPERMAN Created by: JOE SHUSTER and JERRY SIEGEL
...AND THEN, THERE WAS THIS TIME WHEN I GRABBED -- GET THIS --
GROKK, THE LIVING GARGOYLE!
-- BY HIS TAIL AND SWUNG HIM 'ROUND AND 'ROUND UNTIL I LET GO --
-- AND HE SMASHED INTO THIS GREAT BIG BUILDING!

UM...
I imagine there isn't much Clark hasn't seen. He's talked to me about other worlds and even going into the future.
But I don't think he was quite prepared for what he saw today.

MR. KENT, I DON'T READ THE NEWSPAPER ALL THAT OFTEN --
-- BUT, IF I DID, IT WOULD BE YOUR STUFF, FOR SURE.

...WHY ARE YOU HERE?

I'M SURE WHAT CLARK MEANS, SUPERBOY, IS WHAT BRINGS YOU TO OUR LITTLE PLACE?

UM...
...WHY AM I HERE?
Martha, god bless her, would pull a fox out of the hen house with her own two hands if it meant keeping the peace around here.

I JUST WANTED A LITTLE TIME OFF AND--
--I MET YOUR FOLKS A FEW MONTHS BACK AND--
-- THEY TOLD ME THAT ANYTIME I WANTED TO STOP BY FOR SUPPER...
SEE SUPERBOY #8 -- EDDIE.

YOU DID...?
CLARK, YOU MUST BE HUNGRY AFTER YOUR LONG TRIP, WHY DON'T YOU GRAB A PLATE AND --
-- PULL UP A CHAIR AND --

YOU INVITED HIM TO SUPPER?
!

?
YES, CLARK.
HE'S A FINE YOUNG MAN AND HE'S MADE QUITE A NAME FOR HIMSELF, DON'T YOU THINK?

LOOK, MISTER KENT, I SWEAR TO YOU THAT I DIDN'T KNOW YOU'D BE HERE.
IN FACT, NOBODY KNOWS I'M HERE AND, JUST BETWEEN US --
-- I'D LIKE TO KEEP IT THAT WAY.
EVEN THOUGH I KNOW YOU'RE A REPORTER AND STUFF...
WINK
SOMETHIN' ON YOUR MIND, CLARK...?
CAN'T GET A MOMENT'S... ...ACTUALLY INVITED HIM... ...NUTS...
CAN I HAVE SOME MORE OF THOSE BISCUITS AND GRAVY?

I THINK THE DAY WENT WELL, DON'T YOU?
I've learned a thing or three in my life about when something isn't going as expected.
You can plant corn in the same field you've planted it in for years and one day, it just won't work anymore.
Lex Luthor has always been a bit of a burr in my son's side ever since Clark got to Metropolis and my guess is that with all that's happened recently, it hasn't gotten any better.
YES, I --
-- I THINK THE DAY WENT WELL.
IS... DO I SENSE CONCERN IN YOUR VOICE?
CONCERN? ME? HARDLY.
EVEN SUPERMAN, AS MUCH AS I AM LOATH TO ADMIT IT, UNDERSTOOD THE IMPORTANCE OF SQUELCHING PUBLIC CONCERNS.
DELICATE MATTERS.
SIR..?
DELICATE MATTERS NEED TO BE HANDLED DELICATELY.
ALL IT REALLY TAKES IS ONE MALCONTENT--
-- ONE VOICE OF OPPOSITION TO MY INSISTENCE THAT THE CITY IS SAFE --
-- AND THE SHEEP WHO GRAZE HERE WILL SPOOK JUST AS EASILY AS THE DROVES WHO ABANDONED GOTHAM CITY.

BUT...
...YOU'VE TURNED GOTHAM CITY TO *YOUR* ADVANTAGE, SIR.
YES. YES, I HAVE.
AND THAT'S WHY KEEPING ***METROPOLIS*** UNDER MY THUMB BECOMES ALL THE MORE IMPORTANT.
BEING IN CONTROL OF ***TWO*** MAJOR HUBS OF POWER IN THIS COUNTRY--
--REAL POWER --
-- WILL START PEOPLE THINKING THAT LEX LUTHOR KNOWS WHAT'S BEST FOR ALL OF AMERICA.
AND WHO AM I TO ARGUE..?

Clark's told us how good it feels to be back at the Daily Planet. I've never known much about city life, being a farmer...
DAILY PLANET
YOU WANT WHAT?!
...and a father...
I DON'T THINK I COULD'VE SAID IT ANY MORE CLEARLY, PERRY --
-- I COULD USE SOME TIME OFF, TO SORT A FEW THINGS OUT.
LOIS, WE'VE ONLY BEEN BACK UP AND RUNNING FOR A SHORT TIME --
-- AND LOSING MY TOP REPORTER --
-- YOU'VE STILL GOT CLARK.
LOOK, WHEN YOU CAME TO ME TO TALK ABOUT MY MARRIAGE --
-- I ASKED YOU IF EVERYTHING WAS ALL RIGHT AT HOME...
...IS IT?
DIDN'T I SAY WHEN I MADE KENT OUR FOREIGN CORRESPONDENT IT COULD BE HELL ON A MARRIAGE?
DIDN'T I?
SAY THE WORD, LOIS, AND I'LL PUT HIM BACK ON THE CITY BEAT WITH YOU.
WOULD THAT HELP?
WHAT WOULD HELP IS SOME TIME OFF -- OKAY?!
...but I'd have to say there is a certain peace of mind one gets at knowing what chores have to be done tomorrow when you go to bed at night.

FUNERA
FOR A
RIEND
NAL
GHT
HEY, LOIS, GREAT, YOU'RE STILL HERE.
I GOT THOSE SHOTS OF THE LUTHOR/SUPERMAN PRESS CONFERENCE UP ON MY MONITOR AND --
-- AND I THOUGHT WE COULD TAKE A *LOOK* AT THEM --
BUMP
-- OR NOT.
JEEZ.
WHAT'D I DO TO MAKE HER MAD AT ME *THIS* TIME...?

While Clark was growing up, I always thought it was best to take the bull by the horns and face the situation.
Martha, on the other hand, was more than willing to wait the boy out. When Clark was ready to talk about something, that's when they would discuss it.

Later on in life, things start to get a little clearer and I think that both of us now handle Clark differently...
I SAVED YOU A PIECE OF PIE.
THAT BOY HAS SOME APPETITE. REMINDS ME A LITTLE OF --
-- HE'S NOT ME.

OF COURSE NOT, SON. NOBODY COULD EVER BE YOU IN OUR HEARTS.
BUT I'D BE LESS THAN HONEST IF I DIDN'T TELL YOU THAT SEEING HIM THERE --
-- WHAT, HE CAN'T BE MORE THAN SIXTEEN OR SEVENTEEN --
-- BRINGS BACK A LOT OF WONDERFUL MEMORIES.

I JUST DON'T THINK HIS BEING HERE IS A COINCIDENCE.
HE'S BEEN POKING AROUND -- HINTING ABOUT MY... RELATIONSHIP TO SUPERMAN.

ANY PARTICULAR REASON THAT LOIS DIDN'T JOIN YOU FOR THIS VISIT?
NO. WORK. WHY DO YOU ASK?
I -- WE -- JUST HAVEN'T SPOKEN TO HER VERY MUCH SINCE WE SAW YOU TWO AT NEW YEAR'S.

THE TRUTH IS... I DON'T KNOW WHAT'S WITH LOIS LATELY. SHE *CHOSE* NOT TO COME WITH ME.
AND I CAN'T HELP FEELING LIKE SHE MIGHT -- I DON'T KNOW -- SENSE SOMETHING ABOUT WHAT HAPPENED WITH DIANA.
DIANA?
WONDER WOMAN.
OH.
DID SOMETHING HAPPEN WITH... DIANA, CLARK?

I... IT'S HARD TO EXPLAIN, MOM.
TRY.
WE WERE BOTH CAUGHT UP IN A -- MOM, YOU'RE NOT REALLY GOING TO FOLLOW THIS...

IT WAS MAGIC -- BUT IT WAS *NOT* MAGICAL. DIANA AND I GOT SENT TO *ANOTHER DIMENSION.*
WE COULDN'T GET HOME FOR A LONG TIME AND NOTHING HAPPENED BETWEEN US, BUT I STILL DIDN'T THINK IT WAS RIGHT TO TELL LOIS.
HOW LONG IS *"A LONG TIME"*?
ABOUT A THOUSAND YEARS...
A THOUSAND..!

WE *RETURNED* AS IF WE HADN'T BEEN GONE AT ALL AND NOTHING HAPPENED BETWEEN US!
YOU SAID THAT.
SIGH
YOU'RE RIGHT, CLARK, I *DON'T* UNDERSTAND.
BUT, IF *NOTHING* HAPPENED -- OR EVEN IF IT *DID* --
-- YOU'RE SELLING LOIS AWFUL SHORT BY NOT TALKING WITH HER ABOUT WHAT'S WRONG.

THE SAME GOES FOR THAT NICE YOUNG MAN INSIDE...

YOUR MOM ROCKS, MR. KENT.
SHE FOUND ME THESE OLD CLOTHES OF YOURS SO I CAN CRASH HERE FOR THE NIGHT.
PLEASE DON'T TOUCH THAT.

WHO'S THE BABE?
A VERY DEAR FRIEND.
HEY, I REMEMBER MEETING HER! LANA SOMETHING. BUT, SHE WAS OLD -- UM, OLDER THAN IN THIS PICTURE --
-- STILL KINDA HOT THOUGH.

I DIDN'T REALIZE YOU'D BEEN IN SMALLVILLE SO... OFTEN.
ACTUALLY, I'VE BEEN TO THIS SMALLVILLE AND A WHOLE 'NOTHER ONE THAT --
-- WELL, LET'S NOT GO INTO THAT.
DON'T YOU HAVE OTHER RESPONSIBILITIES?

AREN'T YOU PART OF 'YOUNG TEEN JUSTICE LEAGUE JUNIOR TITANS' OR SOMETHING?
HA! YOU CRACK ME UP!
YEAH, I HANG WITH YOUNG JUSTICE -- AND THEY'RE COOL AND ALL --
-- ONLY, IT'S ALL ABOUT BEING A SUPER-HERO WITH THEM, Y'KNOW?

IT'S JUST... SOMETIMES I ONLY WISH I HAD SOMEPLACE WHERE I COULD FALL OFF THE MAP.
KINDA LIKE WHAT YOU DO WHEN YOU COME BACK HERE --
-- I MEAN, WHEN YOU'RE NOT BEING A BIG CITY REPORTER AND ALL.

YOU'RE ON MY BED.

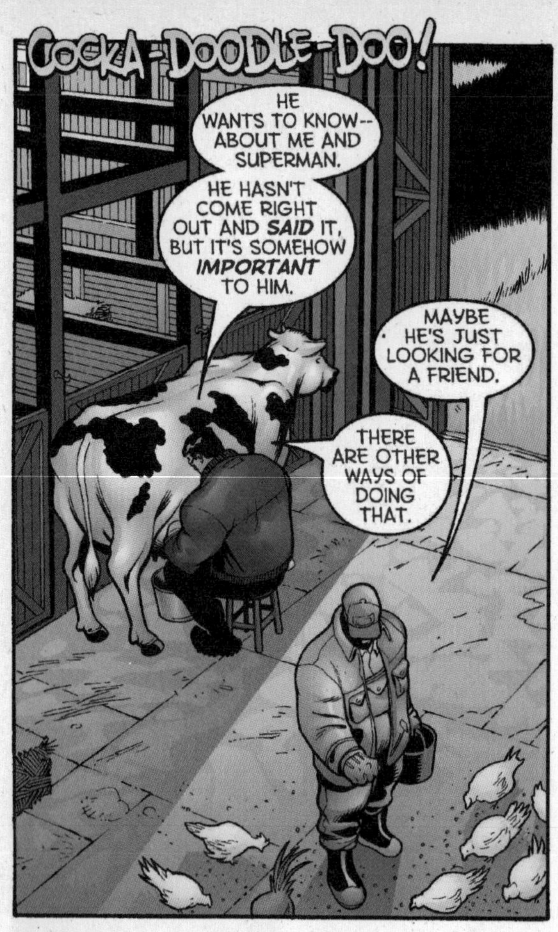
COCKA-DOODLE-DOO!
HE WANTS TO KNOW-- ABOUT ME AND SUPERMAN.
HE HASN'T COME RIGHT OUT AND **SAID** IT, BUT IT'S SOMEHOW ***IMPORTANT*** TO HIM.
MAYBE HE'S JUST LOOKING FOR A FRIEND.
THERE ARE OTHER WAYS OF DOING THAT.

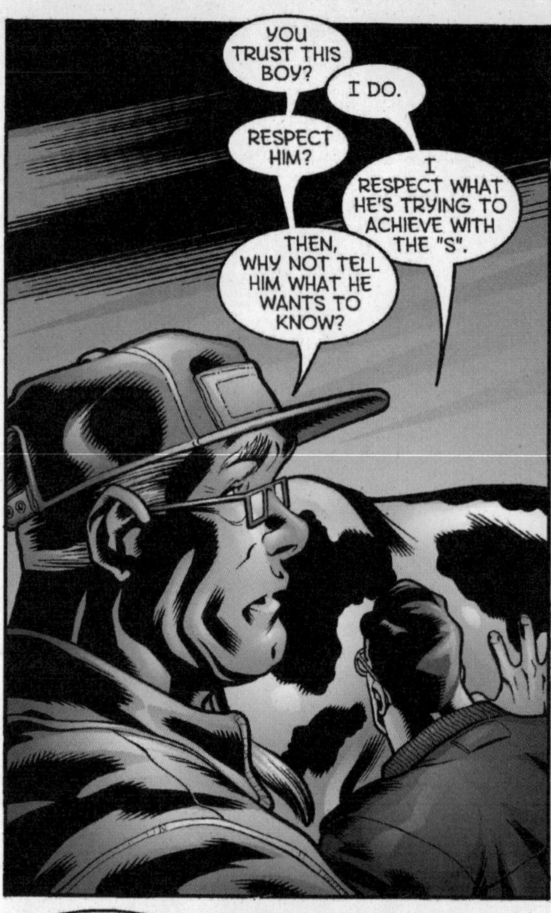
YOU TRUST THIS BOY?
I DO.
RESPECT HIM?
I RESPECT WHAT HE'S TRYING TO ACHIEVE WITH THE "S".
THEN, WHY NOT TELL HIM WHAT HE WANTS TO KNOW?

I REMEMBER WHEN YOU FIRST GAVE ME A PAIR OF YOUR EYEGLASSES.
IT SEEMED LIKE SUCH A SIMPLE THING --
-- BUT JUST BY PUTTING THEM ON, IT PUT UP A BIG ENOUGH WALL FOR ***SUPERMAN*** TO BE ON ONE SIDE --
-- AND ***ME*** TO BE ON THE OTHER.

AND WHENEVER ANYONE LEARNS -- *"THE SECRET"* -- IT CHIPS AWAY AT THAT WALL.
BEING ABLE TO STEP BACK INTO CLARK KENT'S SHOES -- IT'S SOMETHING THAT'S ALL MY ***OWN.***

I'M NOT *TRYING* TO BE SELFISH -- BUT DOESN'T *CLARK KENT* GET TO BE SELFISH ONCE IN A WHILE?
YES, SON. YOU DO. BUT I CAN'T HELP WONDERING...
...THAT BOY -- WITH ALL THOSE POWERS AND ABILITIES --
-- AND HE DOESN'T HAVE ANYONE IN HIS LIFE TO... WELL... SMOOTH OUT SOME OF THE ROUGH SPOTS.
THE PART THAT MAKES US ALL *HUMAN.*

HE DOESN'T HAVE A *"MA AND PA KENT"...*
AND I WOULDN'T BE MUCH OF A SUPERMAN WITHOUT THAT...

JUST SOMETHING TO THINK ABOUT, SON, NOTHING MORE THAN THAT.

YAWN
WHAT'S EVERYBODY DOIN' UP SO EARLY?

HOW'D YOU LIKE TO LEARN TO MILK A *COW?*

TRY IT AGAIN.
GENTLY.

THAT'S IT. I'M DONE!

YOU'RE NOT MUCH WITH PATIENCE, ARE YOU?
NO, IT'S JUST THAT WHEN I SHOULD BE ABLE TO KNOW SOMETHING, I JUST SHOULD.
TELL THAT TO THE COW.

GIVE IT TIME.
EVEN THOUGH IT'S SOMETHING YOU WANT--
-- SOMETIMES IT TAKES THE OTHER PERSON -- OR COW -- TO GET COMFORTABLE WITH IT.

I don't know if Lois and Clark will ever have children.
But, looking out at those two hootin' it up in the barn reminds me of how special it is to have kids around the farm.
YOU WANT TO GIVE IT ANOTHER TRY?
HAVE YOU GOT ANY MORE TOWELS?

SO, YOU HEADED BACK TO METROPOLIS?
I'LL FLY OUT A LITTLE LATER --
-- I THINK MY PLANE LEAVES AROUND NOON.
THANKS, MR. KENT.
I'M GOING TO REMEMBER THIS VISIT FOR A LONG TIME.

IT'S "CLARK," SUPERBOY.
"MR. KENT" IS SOMETHING PEOPLE CALL MY FATHER.

I'M SORRY I KINDA BUSTED IN ON YOUR DAY OFF.
DON'T BE. I'M NOT.

SAVE AN EXTRA BISCUIT WITH GRAVY FOR ME.
YOU FLY SAFELY, NOW.
ANY TIME YOU WANT TO COME BACK--
--YOU'RE ALWAYS WELCOME.
THANKS! I JUST MIGHT TAKE YOU UP ON THAT AGAIN!
NICE BOY.
HE'S GOT SOMETHING, THAT'S FOR SURE.
HOPE EVERYTHING WORKS OUT -- FOR BOTH OF YOU, CLARK.

I *THOUGHT* THAT WAS YOU, ***KON-EL.***
HEADED TOWARD METROPOLIS BY ANY CHANCE?
UH, YEAH.
YOU REALLY GET AROUND, HUH?
YES, I DO. I KEEP PRETTY BUSY -- SOMETIMES SO MUCH I DON'T REALLY GET A CHANCE TO...
...TAKE SOME TIME OFF.

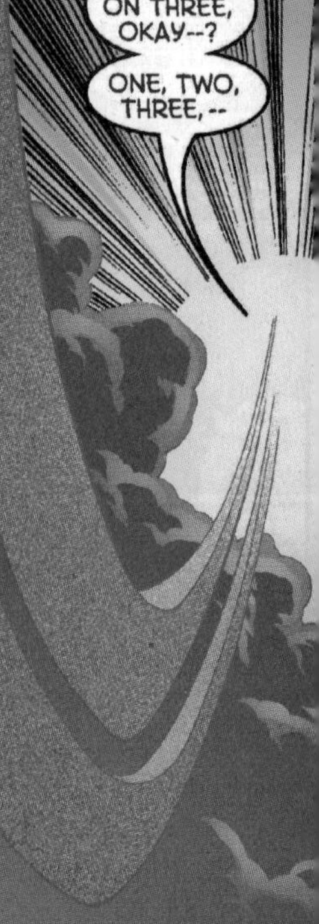

On Sundays, after supper, Clark and I used to go out behind the barn and throw the baseball around.
I kept him on his toes -- curve balls, high and outside, anything that would get him to be able to deal with the unexpected as it came along.
GO!
I'd like to think it has paid off handsomely...

BZZZ BZZZ
I'M COMING--!

OH, IT'S YOU.
WHY DIDN'T YOU USE YOUR KEY?
I THINK I LEFT THEM ON MOM'S KITCHEN COUNTER --
-- ARE YOU GOING OUT SOMEWHERE..?
...AND AREN'T YOU GOING TO BE COLD IN THAT?

I... UM... DIDN'T KNOW WHEN YOU'D BE COMING BACK, SO I MADE PLANS.
DON'T WAIT UP.

SLAM
LOIS...!

DON'T WAIT UP..?

A TALE OF TWO CITIES
HERE, KITTY KITTY...
COME ON, DON'T MAKE THIS DIFFICULT.
I'VE LEAPT TALL BUILDINGS IN A SINGLE BOUND, YOU KNOW.
GREAT SCOTT!
CLARK!
STUART IMMONEN — plot — JAY FAERBER — dialogue — YANICK PAQUETTE and STUART IMMONEN — pencils — RICH FABER and JOSE MARZAN JR. — inks — GLENN WHITMORE and WILDSTORM FX — colors — BILL OAKLEY — letterer — MAUREEN McTIGUE — assoc. ed. — EDDIE BERGANZA — editor —
SUPERMAN created by JERRY SIEGEL & JOE SHUSTER

MY LORD, CLARK! SHOULDN'T YOU BE MORE CAREFUL?
YOU'RE LUCKY NO ONE ELSE SAW YOU, SON. THIS IS SMALLVILLE, NOT METROPOLIS.
PEOPLE HERE PAY ATTENTION TO WHAT'S GOING ON AROUND THEM.

DID YOU TWO ALWAYS WORRY THIS MUCH?

MAMA HERE IS EXPECTING AND I DIDN'T WANT HER TO SET UP HOUSE UNDER THE HOOD OF YOUR PICKUP.

THERE YOU GO, GIRL.
THAT'S STILL NO EXCUSE TO GO FLAUNTING YOUR POWERS. YOU COULD'VE GOTTEN THAT CAT OUT FROM UNDER THE TRUCK ANY NUMBER OF WAYS--
--WITHOUT RISKING YOUR SECRET IDENTITY. WHAT'S GOTTEN INTO YOU, SON?
ANYONE COULD'VE COME OUT OF BENSON'S AND SEEN YOU! YOU'RE JUST LUCKY IT WAS US!
IT HAD NOTHING TO DO WITH LUCK, REALLY. I KNOW YOUR HEART-BEATS, AND THE SOUND OF YOUR FEET.
I'M NO DARK KNIGHT DETECTIVE, BUT I GET BY.
LIL' CHOC

NOW LET'S GO TO THE DRUG STORE AND GET SOME ICE CREAM, OKAY? MY TREAT.
I DUNNO... I STILL NEED TO GET THAT PART FOR THE THRESHER...
PA, I SAID I'D TAKE CARE OF THE THRESHER. I'M GOING TO BE HERE A FEW DAYS, REMEMBER? JUST TAKE IT EASY.

YOU SURE YOU CAN AFFORD TO BE HERE FOR THAT LONG? ARE YOU AVOIDING SOME-THING?
DON'T BE RIDICULOUS, PA. I JUST WANT TO SPEND SOME QUALITY TIME WITH YOU AND MA. LAST TIME I VISITED, SUPERBOY WAS HERE, SO WE DIDN'T GET TO HAVE ANY TIME ALONE, JUST THE THREE OF US.
I GUESS PA HAS A POINT. MAYBE I AM AVOIDING SOMETHING. METROPOLIS HAS CHANGED SO MUCH, THANKS TO BRAINIAC 13.
AND LOIS HAS BEEN ACTING SO DIFFERENT LATELY. I WISH SHE'D TELL ME WHAT'S WRONG.
I GUESS I'M HOPING WHATEVER'S WRONG WILL JUST BLOW OVER WHILE I'M AWAY.
I LOVE IT HERE, YOU KNOW THAT? THE AIR SMELLS DIFFERENT.
IT'S BEEN TOO LONG SINCE I REALLY STOPPED TO JUST APPRE-CIATE WHERE I CAME FROM. AND I LIKE KNOWING THAT NO MATTER HOW LONG I'VE BEEN GONE--
--SMALLVILLE NEVER CHANGES.
GRAY BAKERY
STORE
KANSAS NATIONAL BANK
ICES

CHANGE IS GOOD.
HOPE... MERCY... DID YOU KNOW THAT IF A SHARK STOPS SWIMMING, IT DIES? I'M SURE THERE ARE A LOT OF PEOPLE DOWN THERE WHO WOULD COMPARE ME TO A SHARK.
BUT YOU KNOW SOMETHING? IN A LOT OF RESPECTS, I AGREE WITH THAT COMPARISON.
THERE ARE VERY FEW TIMES IN MY LIFE THAT I'VE EVER BEEN TRULY SATISFIED... THAT I'VE EVER "STOPPED SWIMMING," IF YOU WILL.
BUT HERE, NOW, AS I LOOK DOWN ON METROPOLIS... THIS IS ONE OF THOSE RARE TIMES.
YOUR RIDE IS HERE, MR. LUTHOR.
LOOK. LOOK AT METROPOLIS. MY METROPOLIS.
THE FUTURE IS NOW.
AND I DIDN'T HAVE TO SPEND A DIME.

OH, THIS IS JUST GREAT.
BET YOU HAVE A LOT OF THESE ENVIRONMENTALIST KIDS IN METROPOLIS, eh, CLARK?
YOU THINK THAT POLLUTION WILL JUST GO AWAY IF YOU CLOSE YOUR EYES AND IGNORE IT?
WAKE UP, PEOPLE!
Ah, EXCUSE ME ONE SECOND...
SMALLVILLE
HOT DOG
BURGER
2.00
2.00
1.50
3.00
EARTH-RIGHT-EARTH-RIGHT
HEY, FOLKS. CAN I GET YOU TO SIGN OUR PETITION? ARE YOU AWARE WHAT'S GOING ON OUT AT THE TOWNSEND PLANT?
NOW JUST HOLD ON--DON TOWNSEND'S A GOOD MAN, AND HE DOESN'T NEED ANYONE DRAGGING HIS NAME THROUGH THE MUD!
WE CAME IN HERE FOR SOME ICE CREAM, NOT TO BE ACCOSTED BY SOME--
ICE CREAM? DON'T YOU KNOW DAIRY'S BAD FOR YOU? THEY INJECT COWS WITH STEROIDS THESE DAYS.
AHEM-- WHAT EXACTLY IS THIS PETITION FOR?
TOWNSEND'S PLANT IS VIOLATING ALL KINDS OF E.P.A.♢ REGULATIONS. ME AND MY FRIENDS HERE WANT TO PUT A STOP TO IT.
BUT WE CAN'T DO IT ALONE! WE NEED THE HELP OF THIS TOWN TO DO IT!
--NOT STAGING AN ENVIRONMENTAL COUNTER-ATTACK.
SMALLVILLE SURE HAS COME A LONG WAY SINCE I WAS THIS KID'S AGE.
TEN YEARS AGO, YOU'D FIND THIS SODA SHOP FILLED WITH KIDS TALKING ABOUT THE SCHOOL DANCE, OR CELEBRATING AFTER A FOOTBALL GAME--
♢ ENVIRONMENTAL PROTECTION AGENCY--ED.

WHAT'S YOUR NAME, ANYWAY?
BRETT DECHAMP. WHY?
I DIDN'T RECOGNIZE YOU, AND I THOUGHT I KNEW EVERYONE IN THE COUNTY.
DUDE, I'M NOT FROM SMALLVILLE. ME AND MY BUDS DROVE IN FROM PHOENIX WHEN WE HEARD ABOUT THE PLANT. THE NETWORK SAYS--
THAT'S ABOUT ENOUGH OUT OF YOU, SON.
DON TOWNSEND HERE TOLD ME YOU KIDS WERE TRYIN' TO INCITE SOME KINDA RIOT HERE, BUT I DIDN'T WANNA BELIEVE IT.
HE SAYS THERE'S BEEN SOME VANDALISM AT HIS PLANT, TOO.
THERE'S ALSO A POLLUTED WATER TABLE IN THE SOIL SURROUNDING HIS PLANT. YOU GONNA PUT THAT IN JAIL?
IF SOMETHING HAPPENS TO THAT PLANT, IT WON'T BE BECAUSE OF US!
SHERIFF, PERHAPS WE CAN TAKE THIS DOWN A NOTCH. WHAT DO YOU SAY? BRETT AND HIS FRIENDS ARE TRYING TO DO SOME GOOD.
YOU CALL TRYING TO SHUT DOWN MY PLANT GOOD?!?
SLUSH
TAKE IT EASY, DON. I'LL HANDLE THIS.
THIS AIN'T THE BIG CITY, FELLA. I'M THE LAW HERE, AND I MAKE THE PEACE THE WAY I SEE FIT. WHAT I SAY, GOES.
YOU KIDS HEAR THAT?
GO!

FAR BE IT FROM ME TO TELL YOU HOW TO DO YOUR JOB, SHERIFF, BUT THOSE BOYS HAVE RIGHTS, TOO.
YOU'RE GONNA LECTURE ME ABOUT RIGHTS? WHAT ARE YOU, A LAWYER?
REPORTER, ACTUALLY.
SAME THING, FAR AS I'M CONCERNED. LEMME TELL YOU A LITTLE SOMETHING ABOUT SMALLVILLE.
SMALLVILLE'S A WORKING PERSON'S TOWN, AND WITHOUT IT AND A THOUSAND OTHERS LIKE IT, BIG CITIES LIKE METROPOLIS AND GATEWAY WOULD BE SUNK!
RIGHT-EARTH-RIGHT-
CAL... CAL, TAKE IT EASY. CLARK DIDN'T MEAN ANY OFFENSE, YOU KNOW?
OH, YOU'RE KENT'S BOY? DIDN'T RECOGNIZE YOU. LOOK, I AIN'T A HARD MAN, BUT WE'RE KINDA OLD-FASHIONED AROUND HERE, AND I AIM TA KEEP IT THAT WAY.
GO ON HOME, FOLKS. LEAVE DECHAMP AND HIS BUDDIES TO ME, OKAY?
STILL THINK SMALLVILLE NEVER CHANGES, CLARK?
KEY
LOCKSMITH
I DON'T KNOW, MA... BUT I SURE DON'T REMEMBER SO MUCH HOSTILITY.

YOU SEE THIS? THIS IS WHAT'S GOING TO SAVE YOUR BUSINESS, BELLISARIO.
SAVE MY BUSINESS? MR. LUTHOR, LOOK AROUND YOU, MAN. MY BUSINESS DOESN'T NEED SAVING.
LAST WEEK, I HAD A NICE, RESPECTABLE LITTLE FACTORY OPERATION. NOT TOO BIG, NOT TOO SMALL. NOW LOOK AT WHAT I HAVE TO WORK WITH!
DON'T GET ME WRONG -- I APPRECIATE ALL YOU'VE DONE FOR ME OVER THE YEARS, BUT METROPOLIS IS IN BOOM TIME NOW!
I CAN PAY OFF MY LOAN, AND HAVE MONEY LEFT OVER TO EXPAND! I'M RIDING HIGH!
YOU KNOW WHAT THEY SAY ABOUT HEIGHTS, DON'T YOU? IT'S NOT THE FALL THAT KILLS YOU--IT'S THE SUDDEN STOP AT THE BOTTOM.
I THINK YOU'LL FIND THAT I'M OFFERING MORE THAN THE OPPORTUNITY TO MANUFACTURE A KEY ELEMENT IN OUR FUTURE TOGETHER...
...I'M OFFERING AN OPPORTUNITY TO MAKE HISTORY.
I'M NOT SURE I FOLLOW YOU.
OF COURSE NOT. THAT'S WHY I'M EXPLAINING IT TO YOU.
THE WORLD IS GOING TO COME KNOCKING, WANTING A SLIVER OF WHAT WE HAVE IN THIS CITY OF TOMORROW.
AND THEY CAN HAVE IT-- FOR A PRICE.
DO YOU REALLY THINK I'D LET YOU SQUANDER THIS REAL ESTATE ON YOUR WORTHLESS LITTLE FACTORY?
YOU MANUFACTURE THESE COMPONENTS TO MY EXACT SPECIFICATIONS, AND YOU'LL HAVE A PIECE OF THE EMPIRE.
IF YOU REFUSE--
-- IT'S A LONG WAY DOWN.

THIS LOOKS LIKE A JOB FOR SUPERMAN.
CLARK.
CLARK!
CLARK!
CLARK!!
WHAT'S WRONG, MA?
PLEASE JUST STOP!
HERE, TAKE A BREAK. LET'S GO OUTSIDE.
YOU HEADING OUT, CLARK? I STILL NEED A HAND WITH THAT THRESHER, YOU KNOW.
SURE, PA, I'LL GET--
CLARK KENT, DON'T YOU EVEN FINISH THAT SENTENCE! YOU'RE MY SON, AND I LOVE YOU, BUT I ALSO KNOW YOU--
--AND IF YOU DON'T GET OUT AND DO SOMETHING, YOU'RE GOING TO BURST!
NOT TO MENTION DRIVE ME BANANAS.
DO YOU EVER GET TIRED OF BEING RIGHT ALL THE TIME?

I'LL GIVE YOU A HAND WITH THE THRESHER WHEN I GET BACK, PA!
I FORGET SOMETIMES HOW WELL THEY KNOW ME. I CAN FOOL MOST PEOPLE, BUT NOT THEM.
MA ALREADY WORMED OUT SOME INFORMATION ABOUT WHAT'S GOING ON WITH ME AND LOIS ON MY LAST VISIT.
SHOULD TALK TO PA. GET HIS ADVICE--
--OR MAYBE I COULD JUST CHANGE THE COURSE OF A MIGHTY RIVER, OR SOMETHING.
I DOUBT BRETT DECHAMP AND HIS PALS WOULD APPROVE.
Hmm... SPEAKING OF BRETT AND HIS PALS...

MERCY, HOLD OUR POSITION. SOMETHING HAS CAUGHT MY EYE.
TELLEX
NOW, HOW DOES THIS LOUSY PHONE / ATM WORK?
tap tap tap
MY, MY... WHY SO TESTY, LOIS? AND WHAT A BIG WITHDRAWAL YOU'RE MAKING.
THIS SURVEILLANCE TECHNOLOGY IS PERFORMING BETTER THAN I'D HOPED.
NOW I'LL BE ABLE TO KEEP TABS ON ALL MY "FRIENDS."
WHY NOT JUST TAP INTO THEIR COMPUTERS, SIR?
WHEN I WANT YOUR OPINION, HOPE, I WILL ASK FOR IT. UNTIL I DO, YOU SHOULDN'T SPEAK ON MATTERS WHICH YOU KNOW NOTHING ABOUT.
GET ME OUT OF HERE.
THROOM

TOWNSEND'S PLANT SEEMS QUIET. BUT I GUESS IT SHOULD, CONSIDERING IT'S THE WEEKEND, AND ALL.
OKAY... WELL, THAT KILLED ABOUT TWO MINUTES. NOW WHAT SHOULD I--
--eh? WHAT'S THIS?
GUESS EVERYTHING ISN'T QUIET. LOOKS LIKE BRETT AND HIS BUDDIES. I WONDER WHAT--
SKA-THOOM

I'M TOO FAR FROM ANY SIGNIFICANT BODY OF WATER...

...SO I'LL HAVE TO MAKE DO!

BCB 2737

BLAST IT!

I WAS HOPING TO BE ABLE TO SMOTHER THE FIRE, BUT IT'S SPREADING OUT AROUND ME!

AND IF IT REACHES THE REST OF THE PLANT, BRETT AND HIS PALS MIGHT HAVE THAT ENVIRON-MENTAL CATASTROPHE HE SEEMS TO BE HOPING FOR!

BCB

THAT CLOUD! IT'S TOXIC! IF IT DRIFTS OVER ANY POPULATED AREA, PEOPLE COULD DIE!
BUT BY FLYING IN A TIGHT ENOUGH PATTERN, I'LL HAVE A HOME-MADE VORTEX--
--TRAP-PING IT WITHIN--
--SO THAT I CAN RELEASE IT SAFELY, WHERE IT CAN'T DO ANY HARM.
BUT NOW I'VE STILL GOT A FIRE TO PUT OUT, DOWN AT THE PLANT!

Whew! JUST IN TIME! THIS TRUCK'S CARGO IS HIGHLY FLAMMABLE!
FORTUNATELY, I CAN SCATTER THE REMAINING FLAMES WITH MY SUPER-BREATH.
I'VE GOT TO THINK OF A LESS EMBARRASSING NAME FOR THAT.
THE MAIN FIRE'S OUT, SHERIFF NEUSBAUM! WE COULD PROBABLY USE A FIRE CREW TO MAKE SURE THE FLAMES ARE ALL SMOTHERED, THOUGH.
SUPERMAN, WHAT THE--?!
THEM KIDS HAVE GONE TOO FAR THIS TIME! I'M GONNA SEE THEM ROT IN A CELL UNTIL THEY'RE MY AGE!
I'D BE HAPPY TO HELP IN YOUR INVESTIGATION, SHERIFF. ON THE SURFACE, THIS EXPLOSION DOES NOT APPEAR TO BE ACCIDENTAL IN NATURE.
YOU CAN SAY THAT AGAIN!
I DON'T KNOW WHAT BROUGHT YOU HERE THIS TIME, BUT I KNOW YOU'RE NO STRANGER TO SMALLVILLE.
SO PLEASE DON'T TAKE THIS THE WRONG WAY, BUT I DON'T NEED ANY HELP FROM AN OUTSIDER.

--SO YOU SEE, MR. LUTHOR, BY LETTING US REVERSE-ENGINEER SOME OF THE NEW TECHNOLOGY FOUND IN METROPOLIS--
--YOU'D NOT ONLY MAKE YOURSELF A HEFTY PROFIT, BUT YOU'D ALSO BE CONTRIBUTING SOMETHING TO THIS COUNTRY'S TECHNOLOGY RACE.
I'M SORRY, MR. GATES, BUT WE'RE NOT INTERESTED.
THE PRESIDENT IS ON LINE ONE, SIR.
TELL HIM WE'RE NOT INTERESTED, MERCY.
IS IT NOT ENOUGH I'VE ALLOWED S.T.A.R. LABS TO RELOCATE TO THE CITY TO STUDY THE LONG-TERM EFFECTS OF THE BRAINIAC 13 VIRUS?
PRIME MINISTER HAGGIS IS ON LINE TWO, SIR.
THE SAME GOES FOR THE CANADIANS.
WHO SAID I'M NOT A PATRIOT?
NO MORE CALLS, GIRLS. THIS BORES ME.
DESPITE THE FACT THAT I'VE GOT WORLD LEADERS CALLING IN--
--I'VE STILL GOT A BAD TASTE IN MY MOUTH FROM THIS RECENT "WHO IS SUPERMAN'S WIFE?" BUSINESS.
I THOUGHT FOR SURE THAT GETTING OLSEN'S PHOTO OF SUPERMAN WEARING A WEDDING RING--
--AND RELEASING IT TO THE DAILY PLANET'S BIGGEST COMPETITOR, THE DAILY STAR, WOULD CAUSE THE ALIEN SOME DEGREE OF TROUBLE.
BUT HE APPEARS TO HAVE EMERGED FROM THE ENTIRE INCIDENT UNSCATHED. AS USUAL.
AND TO MAKE MATTERS WORSE, WITH THE UPGRADE, I NO LONGER HAVE AN "IN" WITH THE PLANET.
sigh
HEAD FOR HOME, MERCY.

I DON'T MEAN TO STEP ON SHERIFF NEUSBAUM'S **TOES**--
POLICE-DO NOT CROSS-POLICE-DO NOT CROSS
--BUT I WANT TO MAKE SURE HE DOESN'T **RUSH TO JUDGMENT** IN HIS DESIRE TO ARREST BRETT AND HIS FRIENDS.
A THOROUGH SURVEY OF THE DAMAGE WITH MY **X-RAY VISION** SHOULD TELL ME WHAT I NEED TO KNOW.
SO **ALL** YOU'VE BEEN ABLE TO DETERMINE IS THAT A **BOMB** ON A **TIMER** CAUSED THE EXPLOSION?
POLICE

KID, I KNOW YOU'RE JUST A DEPUTY HERE, BUT YOU'VE GOTTA HAVE MORE TO GO ON THAN JUST A BOMB ON A TIMER.
WHAT KIND OF OUTFIT ARE YOU GUYS RUNNING HERE, RUSSELL?
DETECTIVE CANNELL, I KNOW YOU'RE A HOTSHOT FROM TOPEKA, AND WE'RE REALLY GLAD TO HAVE YOU HELPING OUT ON THIS CASE--
--BUT YOU PROBABLY DON'T WANT TO TAKE THAT TONE WITH THE SHERIFF.
Ah, YES, THE SHERIFF. WHERE IS SHERIFF NEUSBAUM, ANYWAY?
JUST OUT DOIN' MY JOB, Y'KNOW? GOT ME A SUSPECT WITH A MOTIVE, TOO.
DETECTIVE CANNELL, BEHIND ME IS DON TOWNSEND. IT WAS HIS PLANT THAT BLEW UP.
AND THIS CHARMER IS BRETT DECHAMP, OTHERWISE KNOWN AS OUR PRIME SUSPECT.
BRETT AND HIS POSSE HAVE BEEN VANDALIZING THE PLANT, HARASSING THE CITIZENS OF SMALLVILLE, AND JUST BEING AN ALL-AROUND PAIN IN THE NECK.
HE WANTS MY PLANT OUT OF BUSINESS, AND IF THAT HAPPENS, THIS ENTIRE COMMUNITY WILL SUFFER, I TELL YOU!
THE COMMUNITY'S ALREADY SUFFERING BECAUSE OF THE PLANT! YOU GUYS POLLUTE THE GROUNDWATER AND OVERUSE THE AREA'S NATURAL RESOURCES!
IN FACT, I'D--!
GENTLEMEN.
PERHAPS I MAY BE OF ASSISTANCE.
SUPERMAN, I... I THOUGHT I EXPLAINED THE SITUATION TO YOU. WE CAN HANDLE THIS ON OUR OWN.
I'VE NO DOUBT THAT YOU CAN, SHERIFF. BUT AS THE ONLY EYEWITNESS TO THE EXPLOSION, I THOUGHT I COULD SHED SOME LIGHT ON THE MATTER.

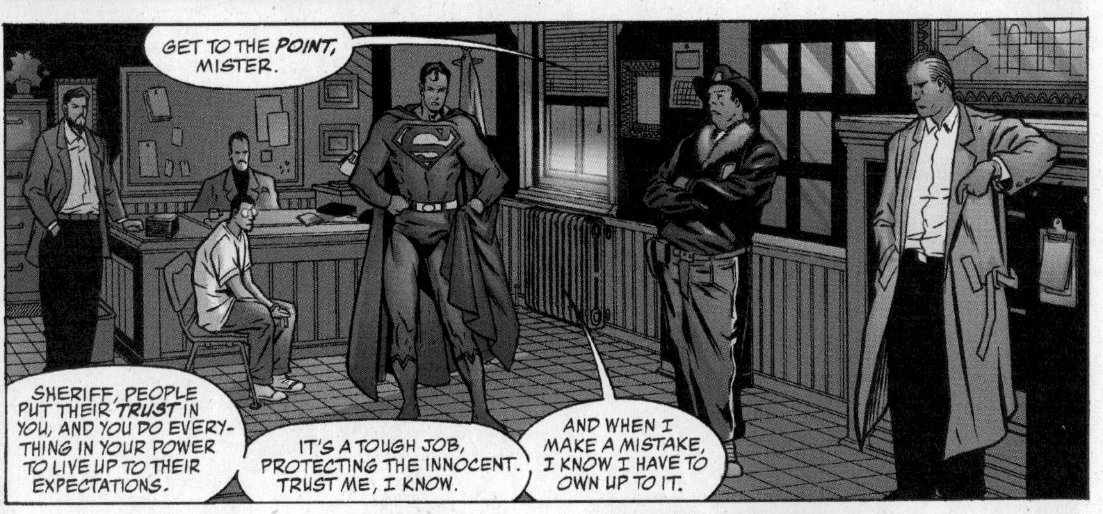

WHAT'RE YOU TRYING TO **SAY?**

I HAVE JUST **ONE QUESTION,** SHERIFF:

DO YOU KNOW HOW TO MAKE **BLACK POWDER,** SIR?

NOW WAIT JUST A MINUTE, SUPERMAN! THAT'S ONE **SERIOUS ACCUSATION,** NO MATTER **WHO** YOU ARE!

WAIT!

HE DIDN'T DO IT ALONE. IT WAS MY IDEA. SHERIFF NEUSBAUM AND I CAME UP WITH THIS PLAN TO FLUSH OUT THE VANDALS.
WE WOULDN'T HAVE PRESSED CHARGES, BUT PEOPLE WERE STARTING TO BELIEVE THE LIES THOSE KIDS WERE SPREADING!
IT HAD TO STOP!
I DIDN'T WANT TO HURT ANYONE, I JUST WANTED TO RUN A BUSINES WITHOUT BEING BOTHERED.
THE BOMB WAS ONLY MEANT TO CAUSE SUPERFICIAL DAMAGE. JUST ENOUGH TO PIN ON THE KIDS.
YOU REALIZE YOUR DAMAGE WENT A LOT DEEPER THAN JUST YOUR OWN BUILDING, DON'T YOU?
TRUST IS A VERY FRAGILE CONSTRUCT, AND IT'S GOING TO TAKE SOME TIME BEFORE SMALLVILLE CAN REBUILD IT.
THANKS, SUPERMAN. YOU'RE ALL RIGHT.
THANK YOU, BRETT. I GREW UP IN A PLACE A LOT LIKE THIS, AND IT'D BE A SHAME IF ANY HARM WERE TO COME TO SMALLVILLE.
BUT IF YOU WERE VANDALIZING PROPERTY, I'D SUGGEST A MORE CONSTRUCTIVE WAY TO GET YOUR POINT ACROSS.
YOU MIGHT BE SURPRISED AT HOW MUCH SUPPORT IS ACTUALLY OUT THERE.
SHERIFF NEUSBAUM'S BEEN IN OFFICE FOR A WHILE NOW.
WHAT COULD MAKE HIM COMPROMISE SMALLVILLE'S TRUST LIKE THAT?
WHEN DID SMALLVILLE START ACTING LIKE SUCH A BIG CITY?

HI, PA.
YOU MANAGE TO WORK OFF ALL THAT EXTRA ENERGY?
YEAH, BUT I CAN STILL HELP YOU WITH THE THRESHER.
THAT'S NOT WHAT I MEANT, SON. EVERYTHING OKAY?

MORE OR LESS.
I LEARNED SOMETHING TONIGHT, PA.

I'VE BEEN AROUND THE WORLD MORE TIMES THAN MOST SATELLITES. I'VE BEEN TO THE EDGE OF THE UNIVERSE, TOO.
BUT DEEP DOWN, I'M THE SAME AS THE NEXT GUY, YOU KNOW? EVERYONE KNOWS SUPERMAN'S NOT HUMAN.
BUT CLARK KENT IS. HE'S JUST A MAN, WITH EARTH IN HIS BLOOD.

WHAT ARE YOU TRYING TO SAY, SON?
THE FARM
I GUESS ONLY THAT THE MORE THINGS CHANGE, THE MORE THEY STAY THE SAME.
WHEN I ARRIVED HERE FROM METROPOLIS, I THOUGHT I'D LOST TOUCH WITH SMALLVILLE.
BUT TONIGHT I LEARNED THAT IT'S JUST CAUGHT UP WITH ME.

"BECAUSE DESPITE ALL THE COSMETIC CHANGE, ONE THING HASN'T CHANGED--

"--IT'S STILL ALL MINE."

SMALLVILLE. THE KENT FARM.
CHAPTER ONE:
ALL THAT DWELL IN DARK WATERS
YOU WERE SAYING, CLARK...?
ABOUT VISITING US WITHOUT LOIS...?
ABOUT HER RECENT BEHAVIOR...?
...HUH... SORRY, MA--PA...
BUT, THE LAKE--FROM THE DIRECTION OF DREAR LAKE...
I HEARD TIRES SCREECHING--A SPLASH...
THERE'S BEEN AN ACCIDENT.
MARK SCHULTZ writer
PABLO RAIMONDI penciller
SEAN PARSONS inker
KEN LOPEZ letterer
GLENN WHITMORE colorist
WILDSTORM FX separations
MAUREEN McTIGUE associate editor
EDDIE BERGANZA editor
SUPERMAN created by JERRY SIEGEL & JOE SHUSTER

MY PERSONAL PROBLEMS ARE GOING TO HAVE TO WAIT.
PA, GET ON YOUR C.B. AND CONTACT EMERGENCY.
...A CAR HAS GONE OFF THE BRIDGE OVE LAKE DREAR!
MA, YOU WERE THE ONE WHO SUGGESTED HE GET OUT OF THE HOUSE MORE OFTEN...
KNOW I SHOULDN'T BE GLAD, BUT ANYTHING TO GET MY MIND OFF MY OWN PROBLEMS...
VERY CURIOUS THAT THERE WOULD BE ANYONE DRIVING WAY OUT HERE AT 5:00 A.M.
WHEN I WAS A KID, I WOULDN'T BE CAUGHT ANYWHERE NEAR LAKE DREAR IN THE DARK...
...AND, AS USUAL, THE PLACE IS FOGGED OVER.
NOT HARD TO UNDERSTAND WHY WE BELIEVED ALL THE STORIES ABOUT THE LAKE BEING HAUNTED.
LET'S SEE IF I CAN CLEAR OUT SOME OF THIS GUNK...
WHY WOULD ANYONE BE DRIVING IN THIS SOUP?!
THERE! MUCH BETTER.
THE DRIVER ZIGGED WHEN HE SHOULD HAVE ZAGGED.

BUT THAT'S NOT MY CONCERN RIGHT NOW...

GOOD! PASSENGER'S CONSCIOUS...
BUT SHE WON'T LAST LONG, EXPOSED TO THIS FREEZING...

LANA!!
WHAT-- HOW...?

LANA-- STAY CALM...

CLA-- SUPERMAN!
SPUTTER!
OH GOD! PETE'S DOWN THERE!
PETE'S DOWN THERE!

STUPID, CLARK!
YOU STAYED TOO LONG WITH HER-- ONE OLD FRIEND OVER ANOTHER-- FORGOT YOUR PRIORITIES...
BUT LANA SHOWING UP NOW?
PETE'S BEEN DOWN AT LEAST TWO MINUTES...
...TIME'S RUNNING OUT.
C'MON, BUDDY! WE THREE HAVE BEEN THROUGH WORSE!
HOPEFULLY, THE LOW WATER TEMPERATURE HAS SLOWED DOWN HIS METABOLISM TO THE POINT WHERE--
--WEIRD-- THE TEMPERATURE--EVEN I CAN FEEL THE COLD...
...AND EVERYTHING'S GONE SO MURK...
SSSUPERMAN...
WHAT IN...

STAY YOUR HAND, SSSSUPERMAN...
UNKETELI CLAIMSSS THISSSS ONE...
UNKETELI, I DON'T KNOW WHO YOU ARE...
...OR WHAT YOUR CLAIM IS...
...BUT IF I DON'T GET THIS MAN TO THE SURFACE...
I HEAR YOUR THOUGHTSSS, I UNDERSTAND YOUR SSSENTIMENTSSS-- BUT THISSS ONE MUSST SSSSTAY...
HE ISSS EVIL...
HE ISSS MINE...
ARRRGH! GREAT... S-SUPERNATURAL...
...UNKETELI MUST BE A SUPERNATURAL BEING--
--THAT'S WHY I FEEL SO WEAK...
YESSS, MORTAL--YOU ARE SSSUSSCEPTIBLE TO MAGICSSSS...
...BUT MY GRIEVANCE ISSS NOT WITH YOU...
UNKETELI ISSS THE SSSSPIRIT OF THISSS LAKE...

...AND A SSSPIRIT OF VENGEANCCCE!
LONG, LONG AGO, MEN-- EVIL, SSSELF-SSSERVING MEN LIKE THISSSS ONE-- DROWNED A YOUNG GIRL IN THESSSE DARK WATERSSSS...
...BUT THE SPIRITSSSS OF THE EARTH TOOK PITY, AND TRANSSSFORMED HER-- THEY WELCOMED HER INTO THEIR COMPANY...
...AND SSSHE BECAME UNKETELI, WHO TAKES THOSSSE WHO WOULD HARM THE INNOCCCCENT...
HSSSSSS-- YOU ARE SSSSTRONG!
STRONG ENOUGH TO KNOW WHEN I'M BEING INTIMIDATED!
UNKETELI, I'M SORRY ABOUT WHAT HAPPENED TO YOU...
...BUT YOU'RE WRONG ABOUT THIS MAN!
SSSSSS

UNKETELI ISSSS NOT WRONG! THISSS ONE ISSSS EVIL!
THE INNOCCCCENT SSSHALL SUFFER!
WHAT COMES ISSS ON YOUR HEAD, SSSSUPERMAN...
ON YOUR HEAD!
HOLY NED! IT'S FORMER CONGRESS-MAN ROSS!
HE'S ONE LUCKY POL, WHAT WITH SUPERMAN HANGING OVER HIS SHOULDER!
WE COULD NEVER HAVE GOT HIM OUT SO QUICKLY...
QUICKLY? QUICKLY?!
HANG IN THERE MR. ROSS!
BUT--THE WATER WITCH--WAS I HALLUCI-NATING?!
WE NEED YOU BACK IN PUBLIC OFFICE WHERE YOU BELONG...

HEY.
HEY.
HAY'S FOR HORSES.

I GUESS WE WERE LUCKY YOU WERE VISITING HOME SAME TIME AS WE WERE.
PETE WILL BE OKAY?

IF YOU MEAN, WILL HE RECOVER FROM THE ACCIDENT...
...YES.
BUT...
BUT...?
CLARK, THERE ARE SOME THINGS SUPERMAN CAN PUT RIGHT, AND OTHER THINGS WE BIG, DUMB HUMANS HAVE TO MUDDLE THROUGH ON OUR OWN.
=SIGH= WE WERE ARGUING, CLARK--FIGHTING WHEN HE LOST CONTROL.
KANSA
WE SEEM TO DO A LOT OF THAT LATELY. DOES THAT SURPRISE YOU?
WELL...
I GUESS I CAN RELATE. THINGS DON'T ALWAYS GO AS PLANNED, DO THEY?
YOU--AND LOIS...?
UM...
SAY, LANA--DID PETE HAPPEN TO REMEMBER--ANYTHING THAT HAPPENED?
DOWN IN THE WATER?
I--I DON'T THINK SO...
SHOULD HE?
PROBABLY NOT.

WHY ARE YOU OUT HERE STARING AT YOUR OLD TREE HOUSE?
IT WAS MY FORTRESS OF SOLITUDE.
MY REFUGE FROM THE WORLD AT LARGE.
I GUESS THAT EVEN AS A KID I FELT DIFFERENT.
EVEN SO, EVERYTHING WAS SO MUCH SIMPLER THEN. SO MUCH CLEARER.
NOWADAYS...
TELL ME ABOUT IT.
BUT, YOU KNOW, CLARK--I'VE ALWAYS THOUGHT OF YOU AS STILL A FARMER AT HEART.
YOU'VE ALWAYS KEPT YOURSELF GROUNDED.
"UNLIKE ALMOST ANYONE ELSE WHO'S BEEN BLESSED WITH GREAT POWER, YOU SEEM TO HAVE NO ULTERIOR MOTIVES...
"...NO PERSONAL AGENDA.
"YOU SIMPLY WANT TO DO THE RIGHT THING.
"YOU WANT TO HELP THINGS GROW."

AM I RIGHT?
I TRY, LANA.
BUT SOMETIMES WHAT LOOKS GOOD IN THE SHORT RUN DOESN'T WORK SO WELL OVER TIME.
YOU KNOW FARMING AS WELL AS I. YOU KNOW THAT ALIEN SPECIES INTRODUCED TO A NEW LAND--WITH ALL THE BEST INTENTIONS--OFTEN DO MORE HARM THAN GOOD.

"ALIEN SPECIES," EH?
WELL, I DON'T HAPPEN TO THINK THAT KRYPTONIANS ARE ALL THAT ALIEN FROM HUMANS.
I THINK WE HAVE MORE IN COMMON THAN NOT.
I THINK YOU PROVE THE POINT.

ABOVE ALL, YOU'RE A FARMER, SUPERMAN.
THE WORLD NEEDS MORE FARMERS.
PETE HAS BEEN FIGHTING HARD FOR LEGISLATION THAT WILL HELP INDEPENDENT FARMERS STAY IN BUSINESS. I KNOW HE'D URGE YOU NOT TO SELL YOUR FARM.
IF IT'S NOT WORKING FOR YOU, REEVALUATE IT--TURN IT INTO SOMETHING THAT'S PRODUCTIVE.

AND DON'T FORGET--I'M ALWAYS HERE FOR YOU.

"RIGHT. MAYBE THE FARMER MUST REALIZE HE'S GROWN BEYOND THE NEED FOR A REFUGE.
"MAYBE HE DOES NEED TO REEVALUATE--TURN IT INTO SOMETHING PRODUCTIVE.
"HE JUST NEEDS TO FIGURE OUT HOW. HOW TO MAKE HIS FORTRESS OF SOLITUDE WORK."

DEEP IN THE BOWELS OF THE *NEW METROPOLIS*...

I'VE GOT ACTIVITY UP AHEAD, TASHA. SWITCHING TO NIGHT VISION, MAGNIFY 8X.

YEAH--IT'S OUR *CYBERNETIC THIEVES* AGAIN.

YOU'VE GOT MY POSITION FIXED?

OF *COURSE*, OH GREAT BLACK HUNTER...

...YOU'RE PEGGED AT SUICIDE SLUM SECTOR DEEP 6, BETWEEN THE 18TH AND 19TH PARALLELS.

WHAT IS THIS--THE *FOURTH* TIME WE'VE RUN INTO THESE WEIRDOS?

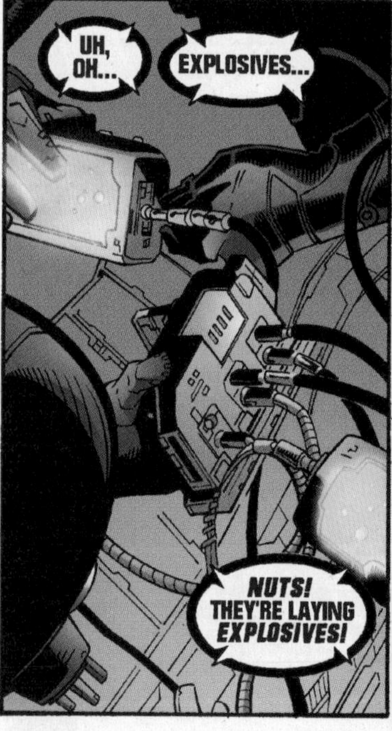

Chapter Two:

In the BELLY of the BEAST

THIS IS NO GAME OF FRIENDLY *TECHNOLOGICAL ESPIONAGE* WE'VE GOT HERE...

...I'M GOING TO BATTLE MODE, TASHA...

TELEMETRY INDICATES THAT BOMB IS *HOT*, UNC!

JEEZ! BE *CAREFUL*-- YOU'RE STILL BREAKING IN A NEW SUIT!

MARK SCHULTZ- writer
DOUG MAHNKE-penciller
SEAN PARSONS-inker
GLENN WHITMORE-colorist
WILDSTORM FX-separations
KEN LOPEZ-letterer

SUPERMAN created by JERRY SIEGEL and JOE SHUSTER

"...THESE DRONES MEAN TO CRIPPLE METROPOLIS' POWER SUPPLY!
BRRRRR
BRRRRR
PING
PING
"I THINK THE RECEPTION PRETTY MUCH PROVES THE INTENT.
PING
PING
PING
"NEW ARMOR IS RESPONDING WELL...
"GAVE ME A CHANCE TO INCORPORATE SOME OF THE INNOVATIONS I'VE BEEN DEVELOPING FOR THE SPECIAL CRIMES UNIT...
TASHA! THE THIEVES ARE PULLING THEIR USUAL FAST FADE...
"DIDN'T HAVE MUCH CHOICE BUT TO START FROM SCRATCH, WHAT WITH ALL ITS PREDECESSORS CORRUPTED BY THE B13 VIRUS..."
...AND WHILE THERE'S NOTHING I'D RATHER DO THAN *NET* ONE OF THEM...

...I'VE GOT TO KEEP MY PRIORITIES IN ORDER.
00:00:25
WHEW. YOU'RE GOING TO HAVE TO HELP ME THROUGH THIS ONE, TASHA.
JUST GET OUT OF THERE, UNC!
GIVE ME A SECOND TO GET MYSELF ORIENTED...
UNC!! GET OUT OF...
THINK MAYBE YOU'RE RIGHT, TASHA...
...THINK MAYBE *DISARMING* ISN'T GOING TO WORK...
PA
TOOM

UNCLE JOHN...?
THE ARMOR IS GOOD, TASHA.
AND LOOKS GOOD, TOO...

...BUT THAT HAD TO HURT.
SORRY I DIDN'T HAPPEN ALONG SOONER, STEEL.
...NOT HALF AS SORRY AS I'LL FEEL IN THE MORNING, SUPERMAN.
HAVEN'T SEEN YOU AROUND THE LAST FEW DAYS.

OH, I'VE BEEN IN AND OUT OF TOWN...
WHAT'S THE STORY ON THE GANG WHO SET THIS UP? I NEVER SAW THEM BEFORE--
--THEY SEEMED TO KNOW THEIR WAY AROUND THIS LABYRINTH.

BETTER THAN I DO.
OUCH. THAT HURTS.
I'VE BEEN HAVING ENOUGH TROUBLE JUST TRYING TO FIGURE OUT THE CHANGES TO MY STEELWORKS, LET ALONE ALL OF SUICIDE SLUM'S...
0010111110011100101110011100
10011111110010100100011111101
01010101001111101010100000101
10101010100000111110101100010
01001010111111100100011010111

...AND THESE CLOWNS-- WHATEVER THEY ARE-- SEEM TO BE WAY AHEAD OF ME.
THEY JUST SORT OF CAME OUT OF THE WOODWORK AFTER THE CHANGE.
THEY APPARENTLY WANT TO TAP INTO THE FLOW OF INFORMATION IN THE NEW SYSTEMS-- WHILE SABOTAGING THE WORKS. GO FIGURE--

--BUT THEY ARE WELL-ORGANIZED, AND, SO FAR, THEY'VE ALWAYS GIVEN ME THE SLIP.
I'M THINKING THEY'RE THINKING WHOEVER DECIPHERS THIS NEW FRONTIER FIRST WRESTS CONTROL OF METROPOLIS FROM LUTHOR.

I'M THINKING THAT'S PROBABLY ABOUT RIGHT.
WHICH ROUNDABOUT BRINGS ME TO THE REASON I HAD NATASHA POINT ME IN YOUR DIRECTION...

MOOSE TO SQUIRREL! MOOOSE TO SQUIRREL!
HOLD ON A MINUTE, SUPERMAN...
GO AHEAD, NATASHA.

WE'VE GOT A SITUATION HERE, UNC...
DON'T WANT TO OVERREACT, BUT... THAT LITTLE RESIDUE CONTAINMENT PROBLEM?
IT'S GONE ALL BALLISTIC.
OR SOMETHING...
JUST HOLD ON, KIDDO—I'M ON MY WAY.
SORRY, SUPERMAN, BUT I'VE GOT TO RUN. TASHA SOUNDED FRIGHTENED-- AND IT TAKES A LOT TO FRIGHTEN THAT GIRL...
I'M RIGHT WITH YOU, JOHN HENRY...

NATASHA MENTIONED A RESIDUE?
ANOTHER MYSTERIOUS GIFT LEFT US BY BRAINIAC 13.
NATASHA AND I WERE BARELY MOVED INTO THE DISTRICT, AND THEN --POOF!--SUICIDE SLUM IS MORPHED INTO SOME SORT OF MONSTROUS POWER GENERATION CENTER.
I'M STILL WORKING TO FIGURE IT ALL OUT.
BUT THE RESIDUE-- THE B13 TRANSFORMATION'S THERMODYNAMIC FLUCTUATIONS SEEM TO HAVE LEFT CERTAIN LINGERING MATTER-ENERGY SIDE EFFECTS THROUGHOUT THE CITY..
I THOUGHT I'D CHECKED THEM ALL OUT TWO WEEKS AGO! THEY WERE WEAK AND FADING...
THEY DID ALL DISSIPATE--EXCEPT FOR ONE PARTICULARLY TENACIOUS BUGGER GROWING OUT OF A GRAVITRON EXPERIMENT IN MY LAB--
--AND OH MY GOD-- I GUESS I DIDN'T DO A VERY GOOD JOB OF CONTAINING IT!

SPONTANEOUSLY GENERATED THERMONUCLEAR GROWTH...
THE FORMATION OF A SUN...?
IT'S OKAY--I'VE GOT YOU NOW!
IT JUST BLEW THE CONTAINMENT CHAMBER WITH ABSOLUTELY ZERO WARNING!
I DON'T WANNA BE HERE...
OR A NEW UNIVERSE.
BUT IT'S NOT FOLLOWING ANY LAWS OF PHYSICS I'M COMFORTABLE WITH. ITS GRAVITATIONAL PULL IS ALL OUT OF PROPORTION...
AND AT THE RATE IT'S GROWING...
IT'S ALREADY THREATENING TO IMPLODE THE STEELWORKS!
...DON'T WANNA ALWAYS BE THE NEWCOMER IN TOWN.
JUST WANNA DO NORMAL TEENAGE STUFF...
...HANG OUT WITH TEENAGERS MY OWN AGE FOR A CHANGE...
A BOOBY TRAP LEFT BY BRAINIAC...?
I DON'T KNOW...
...MAYBE PARTY A LITTLE TOO HARD...

...BUT I DO KNOW THAT I'VE GOT TO GET IT OUT OF HERE BEFORE IT ENDANGERS ALL OF METROPOLIS!
NO! WAIT!

ARRRGH! NOT-- NOT GOING TO WORK...
...HEAT-- IS TOO GREAT...
...NOTHING TO GRAB HOLD OF, ANYWAY...

GET OUT OF THERE, MAN!
GET OUT OF THERE AND LET ME HANDLE THIS!

THAT'S IT! GET CLEAR! I HAVE AN IDEA!
BOMBS AWAY!
CAN I PLEASE GO NOW?

24 TONS OF MOLTEN IRON!
IT'S DESPERATE, BUT THE SUDDEN INFUSION OF THAT MUCH PURE MASS SHOULD SMOTHER THE CHAIN REACTION!
HSSSSS
KRSSSSS

I HOPE YOU'RE RIGHT, STEEL...
...BUT IT LOOKS TO ME LIKE YOU'RE ONLY SPEEDING THE CREATION OF THE ULTIMATE GRAVITY WELL--

--A BLACK HOLE!

WHA...? IT'S OVER...
...IT'S GONE!
JUST LIKE THAT. LUCKY US...
CAN I PLEASE BE EXCUSED NOW?

I DON'T UNDERSTAND...
IT SEEMED TO HAVE EVOLVED INTO THE BLACK HOLE PHASE...
...BUT THEN-- NOTHING. NOTHING AT ALL...

MY...
...MY HAND!

SOME SORT OF SPATIAL DISPLACEMENT..?
NOT QUITE...
I THINK I KNOW WHAT'S HAPPENED HERE. I'VE SEEN THIS BEFORE-- IN THE FUTURE.

FOLLOW ME, JOHN HENRY! IT'S SAFE!
WE'VE JUST WITNESSED THE BIRTH OF...

...A TESSERACT!
A... TESSERACT?
INFINITE SPACE CONTAINED WITHIN FINITE SPACE!
A POCKET DIMENSION!

"JOHN HENRY, I CAME BY TODAY TO ASK FOR YOUR HELP. FOR SOME TIME NOW I'VE BEEN AGONIZING OVER THE PROS AND CONS OF KRYPTONIAN TECHNOLOGY ON EARTH.

"IT COULD DO SO MUCH GOOD IF CONTROLLED AND USED PROPERLY. BUT IF NOT...
"A WISE FRIEND ONCE TOLD ME NEVER TO GIVE UP THE FARM--TO KEEP LOOKING FOR A WAY TO MAKE IT WORK. WELL, I THINK I'VE FINALLY SEEN THE WAY.

"I HAVE THE RAW MATERIALS-- YOU HAVE THE KNOWHOW-- AND NOW I THINK WHAT WE HAVE HERE IS A TRUE SECURITY ZONE."
"JOHN HENRY--WILL YOU HELP ME REBUILD THE FORTRESS OF SOLITUDE?"

CHOOM
CHOOM
CHOOM

:Yawn: BUT I DON'T UNDERSTAND... I WANNA BE IN BED.
SO DOES THE SUN, CLARK... BUT IF HE'S GOTTA GET UP AN GO TO WORK, SO DO WE...

...AND WHAT DID YOU SAY WHEN PAT McBREEDIE CALLED YOU A CHEATER?
I TOLD HIM I NEVER CHEAT. CHEATER CAN'T EVER WIN ...MY PA SAID SO.

WHEN YOU LOOK BACK AT THE NIGHT... THE SNEAKIN' OUT, THE THROWN AXLE, MA'S FACE WHEN SHE GROUNDED YOU AT THREE IN THE A.M.... WAS IT WORTH IT?
ACTUALLY, PA... IT WAS. IT REALLY WAS.

BUT SO... WHEN YOU WANT TO TALK TO A GIRL... AND I'M NOT SAYING THAT I DO, BUT IF A SITUATION HAPPENED BY...
...WHAT DO YOU SAY?
IF I COULD ANSWER THAT ONE, SON... I'D BE A MILLIONAIRE.

PACKED?
YEAH...
GUESS THAT'S IT, THEN? METROPOLIS AWAITS...
METROPOLIS CAN WAIT A FEW MINUTES MORE, PA...

AWFUL QUIET...
WHAT? OH, SORRY...
JUST THINKING... ABOUT SUNRISES.

AND LOIS.
FIGURED.
HEADING BACK TO HER SOON?
SOON.
SOON, SOON?

SHE SAID "DON'T WAIT UP."...
"DON'T WAIT UP," AND SHE DIDN'T COME BACK UNTIL MORNING.

NO DISTANCE FARTHER THAN THE SPACE BETWEEN A HUSBAND AN' WIFE IN AN UNHAPPY BED.
BEEN THERE, SON... WISH I HADN'T, BUT I HAVE.
WHEN THINGS WERE BAD BETWEEN YOU AND MA... WHAT DID YOU DO TO MAKE THEM BETTER?
...

LOOK AT THAT SUNRISE, WOULD YA?

QUIET AFTER THE STORM
JOE KELLY-writer / KANO-penciller / JOE RUBINSTEIN-inker
GLENN WHITMORE & WILDSTORM FX-colors JOHN COSTANZA-letters
MAUREEN McTIGUE-assists / EDDIE BERGANZA-edits
GAS MAIN--
KEEP THOSE BUCKETS MOVIN'!
WHERE'S THE FIRE DEPARTMENT--
LOOK!
SMALLVIL DEPARTMENT STORE
FWOOSH
SUPERMAN!
ALL RIGHT!

SUPERMAN created by
JERRY SIEGEL & JOE SHUSTER
THANK HEAVENS, YOU WONDERFUL--!
GEE... THAT WAS ABRUPT.
WELL, EXCUSE US FOR OUR GENERAL STORE EXPLODING...
FWOOSH
FIFTEEN more seconds to clear out any STRAGGLERS...
Minute and a half to shut down the FLAMES... okay. No BIGGIE... NOT a delay...
TOO BAD. I REALLY was looking for an excuse NOT to go back yet--

I'll just have to--
H-HELP... KOFF-KAFF--
SMASHH
KOFF KOFF
KOFF KOFF
YOU'RE ALL RIGHT NOW, MA'AM... JUST TRY TO RELAX AND--
KAFF KOFF WAIT... MY--
--BABIE...
BABIES!?!
MY BABIES... KAFF PLEASE SAVE MY... BABIES...
HOW COULD I MISS--
MA'AM... I'M LOOKING THROUGH THE APARTMENT AND...
THERE'S NO ONE ELSE IN THERE. I PROMISE... EVERYTHING'S ALL RIGHT--
NO! MY BABIES!!! PLEASE!
OH...
BUT... THERE AREN'T ANY BABIES...

LET ME REPEAT MYSELF, SO THAT THERE IS NO CONFUSION.
--YOU WILL BE APPROACHED BY REPORTERS. YOU WILL BE APPROACHED BY LAW ENFORCE-MENT.
YOU WILL BE HOUNDED BY FAMILY AND FRIENDS FOR GOSSIP TO SPICE UP THEIR OTHER-WISE TEDIOUS LIVES.
THERE AREN'T ANY BABIES IN LEXTOWER...
THE ANSWER IS ALWAYS THE SAME.
YOU NEVER SAW THE CHILD.
YOU KNOW NOTHING ABOUT THE CHILD.
OUR BENEFACTOR HAS SUFFERED A TERRIBLE LOSS. THIS IS HOW HE HAS CHOSEN TO PROCESS IT.
AND AS FAR AS ANY OF YOU ARE CONCERNED-- THERE NEVER WERE--
WE OWE IT TO HIM TO PRESERVE HER MEMORY HIS WAY.
YOU WOULD DO BETTER TO SEW YOUR MOUTH SHUT WITH BARBED WIRE THAN TEMPT ME ON THIS.
DISMISSED.
ARE YOU READY, SIR?
...
YES. IT'S TIME.
OPEN IT.

OPEN IT.
GO ON.
...
AND WHAT'S THAT SUPPOSED TO BE? MAGIC BOX OF HAPPINESS FROM YOUR AMAZON PAL?
LOIS... IT'S... IT'S JUST A LITTLE SOME-THING... OPEN--
I'M NOT INTERESTED IN LITTLE, CLARK.
LITTLE DOESN'T CUT IT FOR ME. YOU WANT ME...
--THINK BIG.
LOIS... PLEASE... TALK TO ME.
SLAM
OR DON'T THINK OF ME AT ALL.
"LOOK AT THAT SUNRISE, WOULD YA?"

PA, I'VE SEEN THE SUNRISE A MILLION TIMES...
I'VE EVEN SEEN IT FROM THE MOON...
IT DOESN'T HELP ME WITH LOIS.
A MILLION TIMES... THAT'S A LOT OF TIMES...
BUT IT'S STILL BEAUTIFUL, ISN'T IT? FIRE RUBY IN THE SKY. CLOUDS LIKE NOWHERE ELSE-- 'SPECIALLY THE MOON-- RIGHT?
SURE... YEAH... IT'S GORGEOUS...
A MILLION TIMES, AND STILL BEAUTIFUL, BUT ONLY WHEN YOU REMIND YOURSELF TO SEE IT.
WHEN TIMES GET ROUGH WITH MA AND ME... WHEN IT FEELS LIKE WE'RE HOEING THE SAME ROW FOR THE MILLIONTH TIME...
...I REMIND MYSELF OF ALL THE LITTLE THINGS THAT MAKE ME LOVE HER.
LITTLE THINGS ALWAYS BRING US BACK TO THE TABLE... AN FROM THERE, THE BAD LOOKS A LOT MORE MANAGEABLE, I PROMISE.
SOUNDS GREAT...
BUT WHAT IF THE LITTLE THINGS DON'T WORK?
NOTHING SEEMS TO WORK...

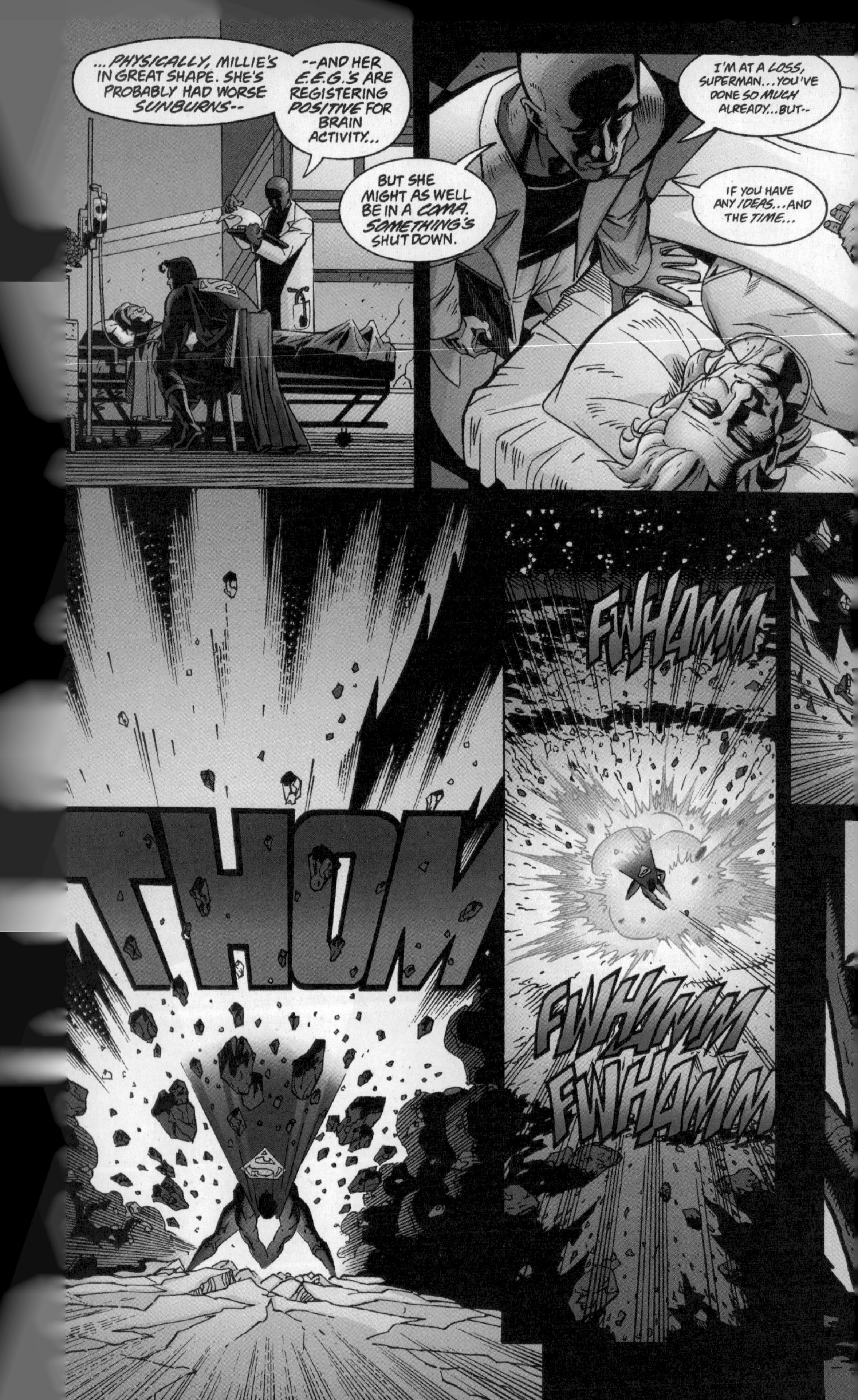
...PHYSICALLY, MILLIE'S IN GREAT SHAPE. SHE'S PROBABLY HAD WORSE SUNBURNS--
--AND HER E.E.G.'S ARE REGISTERING POSITIVE FOR BRAIN ACTIVITY...
BUT SHE MIGHT AS WELL BE IN A COMA. SOMETHING'S SHUT DOWN.
I'M AT A LOSS, SUPERMAN...YOU'VE DONE SO MUCH ALREADY...BUT--
IF YOU HAVE ANY IDEAS...AND THE TIME...
THOM
FWHAMM
FWHAMM
FWHAMM

I'LL MAKE THE TIME, DOCTOR... BESIDES...
I'M IN NO REAL RUSH TO GET HOME.
HYYEARRRGH
SAD, ISN'T IT?
LANA?
HEY, CLARK... HOW-- SNF
OH BOY-- YOU HAVE TO BELIEVE I WAS TRYING REALLY HARD NOT TO COLLAPSE IN FRONT OF YOU-- SNF
LANA... WHAT ARE YOU DOING HERE? IS PETE--?
SLEEPING. PAIN KILLERS... HE'S OKAY, CONSIDERING...*
I SAW YOU AT THE HOSPITAL IN YOUR... BUSINESS SUIT. WHEN YOU DIDN'T STOP IN, I THOUGHT YOU MIGHT SWING BY HERE.

I'M SORRY, LANA... I'VE BEEN MEANING TO SEE PETE...
IT'S JUST BEEN... IT'S BEEN A REAL DAY.
I KNOW... PLUS... YOU'VE GOT A LOT ON YOUR MIND... LOIS...
WE'RE GOING THROUGH SOMETHING... YES.

...
...
I'M FOCUSING ON THE MILLIE PROBLEM RIGHT NOW... SHE MENTIONED "BABIES"--
THAT'S WHY I CAME BY. YOU DON'T KNOW MILLIE, SHE MOVED BACK HERE AFTER YOU LEFT. SHE JUST ADORES CHILDREN...

SOMEHOW, THIS TRADITION STARTED--YOU KNOW HOW SMALLVILLE LOVES A TRADITION...
WHEN YOU HAVE A BABY, YOU BRING MILLIE THE FIRST EMPTY JAR OF FOOD, AND SHE SAYS A PRAYER OVER IT.
baby

GOOD LUCK, THEY SAY... IT'S SILLY... BUT PRACTICALLY EVERYONE IN SMALLVILLE'S GIVEN HER A BABY JAR.
LITTLE CLARK WAS GOING TO PAY HER A VISIT THIS WEEK, BUT...WELL, YOU KNOW HOW THAT TURNED OUT.

PETE DIDN'T WANT TO MISS IT.
SNF SO STUPID, ISN'T IT... SOMETHING SO SMALL CAN GET TO YOU...
IT'S NOT STUPID, LANA... IT'S... IT'S SPECIAL.

AND IT'S GIVEN ME AN IDEA... SEE YOU LATER?
SURE... LATER, CLARK. ALWAYS LATER.

YOUR FATHER'S GOING TO RAISE HECK IF YOU MESS WITH THAT TRACTOR.
NOT IF WE WORK ON IT TOGETHER. DOING CHORES "WITH" INSTEAD OF "FOR" PA GOES A LONG WAY.
YOU WOULD HAVE SHOT OVER, AN' WE WOULDN'T HAVE BEEN ALONE LONG ENOUGH FOR YOU TO TALK ABOUT YOUR TROUBLES.
YOU DO WANT TO TALK... AM I WRONG?
...

I DO... AND I DON'T. IT'S TOUCHY. IT'S...
WHEN YOU AND DAD DIDN'T GET ALONG SO WELL... WHAT DID YOU DO TO MAKE IT BETTER?

IN A NUTSHELL, CLARK, WE TALKED. ALL THE TIME, 'SPECIALLY WHEN SOMETHING TROUBLESOME CAME UP.
WASN'T ALWAYS EASY. YOUR FATHER LIKED TO START THE BALL ROLLING WITH LITTLE GESTURES.
HE'S A ROMANTIC, BELIEVE IT OR NOT.

MM-HMM... LIKE THE THRESHER INCIDENT. WELL, DINNER'S ON IN THREE MINUTES.
YOU DIDN'T HAVE TO COME ALL THE WAY OUT HERE, MA. YOU COULD'VE WHISPERED FROM THE ROOT CELLAR, I WOULD HAVE--

AND TALKING WAS ENOUGH?
HA! HARDLY! TIMES WE FOUGHT LIKE PIGS OVER A MUDPATCH, AND NOTHING WORKED!
SO WHAT DID HE DO THEN?

WELL, HMMM... I SHOULD REALLY LET HIM TELL YOU, CLARK...
HE DOESN'T THINK I KNOW, AND IT WOULDN'T BE RIGHT FOR ME TO SAY.
KNOW WHAT?

CLARK KENT, WHAT DID I JUST SAY?
NOW GET IN HERE AND WASH YOUR HANDS, AND TOMORROW, TALK MAN TALK WITH HIM YOURSELF.
OKAY, MA. OKAY.

WHAT'S HE UP TO?
BOMB?
ALIEN INVASION?
NATIONAL WHISPER.
SUPERMAN?
SUPERMAN? I CAME AS QUICKLY AS I COULD... IS EVERYTHING ALL RIGHT?
THAT'S ONE.
YOUR BIRTH RECORDS ARE ALL CURRENT, RIGHT?
OF COURSE.
GREAT.
I WAS WONDERING IF YOU WOULDN'T MIND GATHERING UP SOME FOLKS WHILE I WORK A LITTLE OUT HERE...
MILLIE...? MILLIE? PLEASE OPEN YOUR EYES...
I FOUND YOUR BABIES.

OH... OH MY...
ALL OF THEM.
I COULDN'T DO TOO MUCH ABOUT THE LABELS, BUT I SIFTED OUT THE GLASS AND MATCHED IT UP BY MOLECULAR--WELL, IT DOESN'T MATTER...
I PROMISE YOUR BABIES ARE OKAY... THE GLASS ONES AND THE REAL ONES.
THEY... THEY CAME HERE... FOR ME?
I... I DIDN'T KNOW... ANYONE CARED.
LITTLE THINGS, MILLIE... LITTLE THINGS...

DONE.
YOUR ATTENTIVENESS IN THIS MATTER HAS BEEN EXEMPLARY, LADIES.
LET LOOSE THE HOUNDS.

MISTER LUTHOR, OFFERS STREAMING IN FROM JAPAN --
TELEPHONE UPLINKS STEADY, BUT PEOPLE DEMANDING CABLE--
ENERGY OUTPUT UP 3000%
--DISCOVERED THE MANHOLES ARE A NEW METAL--
PRESIDENT ON LINE ONE
YEAH, CENTRAL? THIS IS FRANKLIN...

JUS' CHECKIN' IN ON THAT WORK ORDER. MISTER LUTHOR TOOK HIS TIME...
PFSHHHHH
YEP. ON IT NOW...

ONE NURSERY, SEALED.
BYE-BYE, BABY.

WHAMM
CLARK!
WHAT DO YOU THINK YOU'RE--
SWOOOOOSH
METROPOLIS AIR SPACE MUSEUM
--DOING?

IS THAT... IS THAT THE CONSTITUTION?
...
WE SHOULDN'T BE HERE. TAKE ME BACK, CLARK. WE DON'T KNOW IF THIS BUILDING HAS BEEN CHECKED SINCE THE UPGRADE AND--
OH...
LOIS, I WOULDN'T NORMALLY ASK THIS, BUT WOULD YOU PLEASE JUST SHUT UP AND PLAY ALONG?
WHAT DID YOU DO? WHAT IS THIS--?
PLEASE.
LOIS...
...LOIS, I'M LOSING YOU.
I DON'T KNOW WHY. I DON'T KNOW HOW... BUT I'M LOSING YOU, AND I WANT IT TO STOP.
SO I'M TAKING YOU BACK TO WHERE IT BEGAN, SO WE CAN START OVER...
AND MAKE SURE WE GET IT RIGHT THE SECOND TIME THROUGH.
CLARK...
OPEN YOUR PRESENT.

MY OLD TAPE RECORDER? WASN'T THIS SITTING IN A DRAWER SOMEWHERE, BROKEN?
YES. UNTOUCHED BY THE VIRUS. I HAD IT FIXED UP.
WHY? I HAVEN'T INTERVIEWED WITH A RECORDER FOR AGES--
I KNOW, BUT YOU DID, ONCE. TO SECRETLY TAPE YOUR FIRST CONVERSATION WITH SUPERMAN.
HEH... YES...YES I DID.
SO I THOUGHT, MAYBE... WE COULD USE IT TOGETHER. TO TALK. INTERVIEW EACH OTHER ABOUT EVERYTHING AND ANYTHING.
AND MAYBE, SOMEWHERE ON THAT TAPE...WE CAN FIND US AGAIN.
WHATEVER'S WRONG, WE CAN FIX IT, LOIS. I KNOW WE CAN. JUST TALK TO ME.
JUST TALK.
...
KLIK
I NEED TO BE AWAY FROM YOU FOR A WHILE.

BUT WHAT IF THE LITTLE THINGS DON'T WORK?
HEH... WELL... SOMETIMES, EVEN THE SUN WON'T MAKE A ROOSTER CROW.
YOU WAIT IT OUT.

DON'T TELL YOUR MA... BUT WHEN WE'D GET JUST ORNERY AT ONE ANOTHER, AND NOTHIN' WORKED AND I COULDN'T TAKE IT ANYMORE...
I'D HEAD OUT BACK AND BREAK STUFF.
BARE KNUCKLES. BLOOD AN' SPLINTERS. I'D JUST BREAK IT ALL.

DID IT WORK?
NAH. NOT REALLY... BUT IT WAS SOME-THING TO DO UNTIL YOUR MOTHER FIXED THINGS.
AND YOU KNOW WHAT?

SHE ALWAYS DID.
THANKS, PA... I'LL GIVE IT A SHOT.
ANY TIME, CLARK... ONLY MIND WHAT I SAID 'BOUT KEEPING MY LITTLE SECRET BETWEEN YOU, ME AN' THE SUNRISE...
...MA THINKS I'M GENTLE AS A LAMB... I WOULDN'T WANT HER DISAPPOINTED.

HFFF
PUFF
HUFF
I HOPE YOU FEEL BETTER.
ANOTHER FIFTEEN MINUTES AND YOU'D HAVE KNOCKED US OUT OF ORBIT.
WANT TO TALK ABOUT IT?
NO. THANK YOU, J'ONN...
MIGHT HELP, AND A LOT LESS PAINFUL. YOU CAN NOT MAKE YOURSELF BLEED ON MOONROCK, BUT I'M SURE THAT DID NOT TICKLE.
TRUST ME... THIS DOESN'T HURT AT ALL COMPARED TO... WELL, COMPARED TO--
DON'T WORRY... I'M OKAY... I'M--
I--KAFF-
I'M-KOFF
KOFF--KAAF
KAL EL--?
I--KAFF--
I THINK MAYBE...
MAYBE I'M NOT OKAY AFTER ALL.

"-- AND IT WAS ONLY THEN, THE BANK ROBBERS -- THAT IS CORRECT, ORDINARY *BANK ROBBERS* -- OPENED FIRE ON THE MAN OF STEEL.

"THE BULLETS, OF COURSE, BOUNCED OFF HIS CHEST, AND THEN WERE CAUGHT BY SUPERMAN HIMSELF SO AS NOT TO ENDANGER ANY INNOCENT BYSTANDERS.
FAP FAP FAP FAP FAP FAP FAP FAP FAP FAP FAP FAP FAP FAP
BUDDA BUDDA BUDDA
THE Tender Trap
JEPH LOEB Writer
ED McGUINNESS Pencils
CAM SMITH Inks
TANYA & RICHARD HORIE Colors
RICHARD STARKINGS & COMICRAFT Letters
MAUREEN McTIGUE Associate Editor
EDDIE BERGANZA Editor

BANK
KKLICK
"WITHIN MOMENTS, THE BANK ROBBERS FOUND THEMSELVES OUT OF AMMUNITION AND SUPERMAN MOVING IN ON THEM.
FWING
"THEY PANICKED, UNCERTAIN WHAT TO DO. FAILURE, HOWEVER, WAS THEIR ONLY OPTION.
-NNGGNN-
PLINK
"THIS WAS CLEARLY NO WORLD-THREATENING SUPER-VILLAIN AND, AT LEAST FROM THIS REPORTER'S VANTAGE POINT, SUPERMAN DID NOT EVEN BREAK A SWEAT.
Superman created by JERRY SIEGEL and JOE SHUSTER

"WHICH BRINGS US TO THE QUESTION: WHY WAS SUPERMAN HANDLING AN ORDINARY BANK ROBBERY IN THE FIRST PLACE?
SKERUNCH
-HUFF- -HUFF- -HUFF-
"THE METROPOLIS POLICE DEPARTMENT WERE ALREADY ON THE SCENE AND PROBABLY COULD HAVE DEALT WITH IT.
"WHILE NO ONE WOULD EVER DENY THAT SUPERMAN'S CHOSEN ROLE IS TO PROTECT INNOCENT LIVES, NO MATTER HOW LARGE OR SMALL THE SITUATION --
THUNK
"-- STORY CONTINUES ON PAGE 13...
RRRRR
RRR

"...CONTINUED FROM PAGE 1.
THE ENTIRE MATTER SEEMED
A BIT LIKE USING A CANNON
INSTEAD OF A FLY-SWATTER.
LOIS LN
JONES ST
NO
Shuster

"SO IF YOU ARE EVEN THINKING ABOUT BREAKING THE LAW IN METROPOLIS, THINK AGAIN.
"BECAUSE, FOR WHATEVER REASON, SUPERMAN HAS A MAD ON."
GOOD STUFF. I LIKE THE CANNON AND FLY SWATTER.
BUT... WHAT'S THE ANSWER? WHAT COULD GET BIG BLUE SO RILED?
DAILY PLANET
NO SWEAT!

HMMM...?
CLARK, WHILE I *DO* APPRECIATE YOU COVERING THE *CITY BEAT* WHILE LOIS -- WELL -- *FOR* LOIS --
I *DID* SEND YOU TO SIBERIA TO COVER THAT AVALANCHE --
IT'S ON YOUR DESK ALREADY.
WHAT?!

OH, IT IS, ISN'T IT...
BERIAN
ALANCHE
DISASTER
l Pipeline in
nger, Hundreds
Workers Injured
By Clark Kent
1300 words

I like Clark Kent. Always have, from the first day I met him. He writes the way he is -- from the heart.

I usually don't like to pry into the personal affairs of the people who work for me, but Clark -- and Lois, even more so -- mean an awful lot to me.
An awful lot.
DRY CLEANERS CLOSED BEFORE YOU COULD GET THERE?
SHUD
KLICK

I...
OR WERE YOU SLEEPING ON YOUR COUCH?
HOW DO YOU...?

I'VE BEEN A NEWSPAPERMAN, KENT, FOR FORTY YEARS, MAN AND BOY.
THE DEVIL IS ALWAYS IN THE DETAILS.
NOW, EITHER LOIS HAS YOU SLEEPING ON THE COUCH OR --
-- YOU'VE BEEN ROLLING UP THAT SHIRT INTO A LITTLE BALL AND STICKING IT INTO YOUR POCKET.

I WARNED YOU BOTH THAT THIS FOREIGN CORRESPONDENT JOB WOULD BE HARD ON A MARRIAGE --
-- I WISH IT WERE AS SIMPLE AS THAT, PERRY.

THINK SHE'S SEEING ANYONE?
WHY WOULD YOU ASK THAT?
IT'S WHAT WE DO AROUND HERE, CLARK.
WE ASK THE TOUGH QUESTIONS EVEN WHEN WE DON'T WANT TO.
NO. I DON'T THINK SHE'S SEEING ANYONE.
ARE YOU SEEING SOMEONE ELSE?
NO!
GIVE HER ANY REASON TO THINK SO?
NO.
Not the strongest denial I've ever heard. I'd hate to think that Clark has done something -- knowingly or otherwise -- to hurt Lois.

WELL... I'M SURE IT'S NOTHING MORE THAN "GROWING PAINS."
PERRY WHITE PUBLISHER
GROWING PAINS.
EVERYONE GOES THROUGH 'EM, KENT.
THE SIGN OF A GOOD MARRIAGE ISN'T HOW YOU FARE THROUGH THE GOOD TIMES --
-- IT'S HOW YOU DO DURING THE BAD ONES.
LOIS...?
LOIS LANE
NOW, THAT'S A MISTAKE YOU HAVEN'T MADE IN A LONG TIME.
LOIS LANE
LANA...?!
Lana Lang. Clark's high school sweetheart.
This is one of those days I'm glad I ONLY run a newspaper.

WHAT ARE YOU DOING HERE? HOW'S THE BABY?
THE BABY IS FINE. GIVING PETE A LITTLE "QUALITY" TIME WITH HIM.
PETE'S JUST RECUPERATING AT HOME AFTER HIS... ACCIDENT.

AND I CAME TO SEE YOU, CLARK.
METROPOLIS ISN'T EXACTLY THE NEXT FARM OVER.
ALTHOUGH FROM THE LOOK OF THINGS, METROPOLIS ISN'T TH METROPOLIS I REMEMBER A FEW MONTHS AGO!

I... KNOW, BUT IT'S USUALLY ME WHO COMES OUT TO SMALLVILLE --
LAST TIME YOU WERE THERE, WE TALKED ABOUT YOU AND LOIS...
... AND... I GOT A LITTLE WORRIED.

THERE'S NOTHING TO BE WOR-- KAFF-KAFF-KAFF
KAFF KAFF KAFF
CLARK?!

WHAT? I'VE GOT A LITTLE COUGH!
MAYBE I'M COMING DOWN WITH A --

-- COLD...?
CLARK, YOU DON'T COME DOWN WITH ANYTHING --

WELL. ISN'T THIS HOMEY.
WHAT'S THE MATTER, LANA? BABY CLARK NOT AS FUN AS BIG CLARK?
HEY, IT'S GREAT TO SEE YOU --
SAVE IT. THAT'S MY DESK YOU'VE GOT YOUR BUTT PARKED ON.
LOIS...!
When Lois first interviewed for the job, I could tell she had the stuff.
She was something back then. All spitfire and wildcat. Nobody could or would tell her where to get off.
LOIS, WHERE HAVE YOU BEEN?
WORKING. OUT. THINGS YOU WOULDN'T UNDERSTAND.
TRY ME.
WHATCHA GOT THERE?
LUTHOR'S PERSONAL FINANCIAL RECORDS...?
LOOK, IT'S MY DESK.
MY WORK.
MY STORY.
AND MY HUSBAND.
AT LEAST, FOR NOW.
EXCUSE ME --?
IT WAS NICE SEEING YOU, TOO.

HOW CAN YOU MAKE A JOKE?
CAN'T YOU SEE WHAT SHE'S ACTING LIKE? SHE'S LIKE SOMEBODY ELSE!
I'M SORRY... BUT I'M NOT ABOUT TO LET ANYBODY SPEAK TO ME LIKE SHE DID.
LANA, I'M SORRY, TOO. THIS WHOLE... THING HAS ME GOING IN CIRCLES.
I DON'T KNOW WHAT TO DO NEX--
HAALLLLPP!
--T...!
LANA.
I'LL BE RIGHT BACK.
WAS THAT OLSEN WHO JUST WENT FLYING BY?!

When Superman came onto the scene, I watched as slowly, some of Lois's edge came off.
I'd never tell her this, but I remember her slipping up one night and calling him her "Prince Charming."
TAKING UP FLYING, JIM?
Lois was never very good about being vulnerable around men, and keeping company with someone who was invulnerable made it only worse for her.
I WAS COMIN' INTO WORK AND HE COMES OUTTA NOWHERE -- HE TOLD ME HE WANTED TO FIND YOU -- BUT I TOLD HIM, I DON'T KNOW WHERE YOU HANG OUT --
-- BUT HE INSISTED THAT IF ANY OF YOUR FRIENDS WERE IN DANGER, YOU'D COME RUNNING, AND --
-- AND IT WAS WEIRD, LIKE HE KNEW ALL ABOUT ME --
JIM, CALM DOWN. WHO ARE YOU TALKING ABOUT?
PARA--
--SITE...!
WHOM

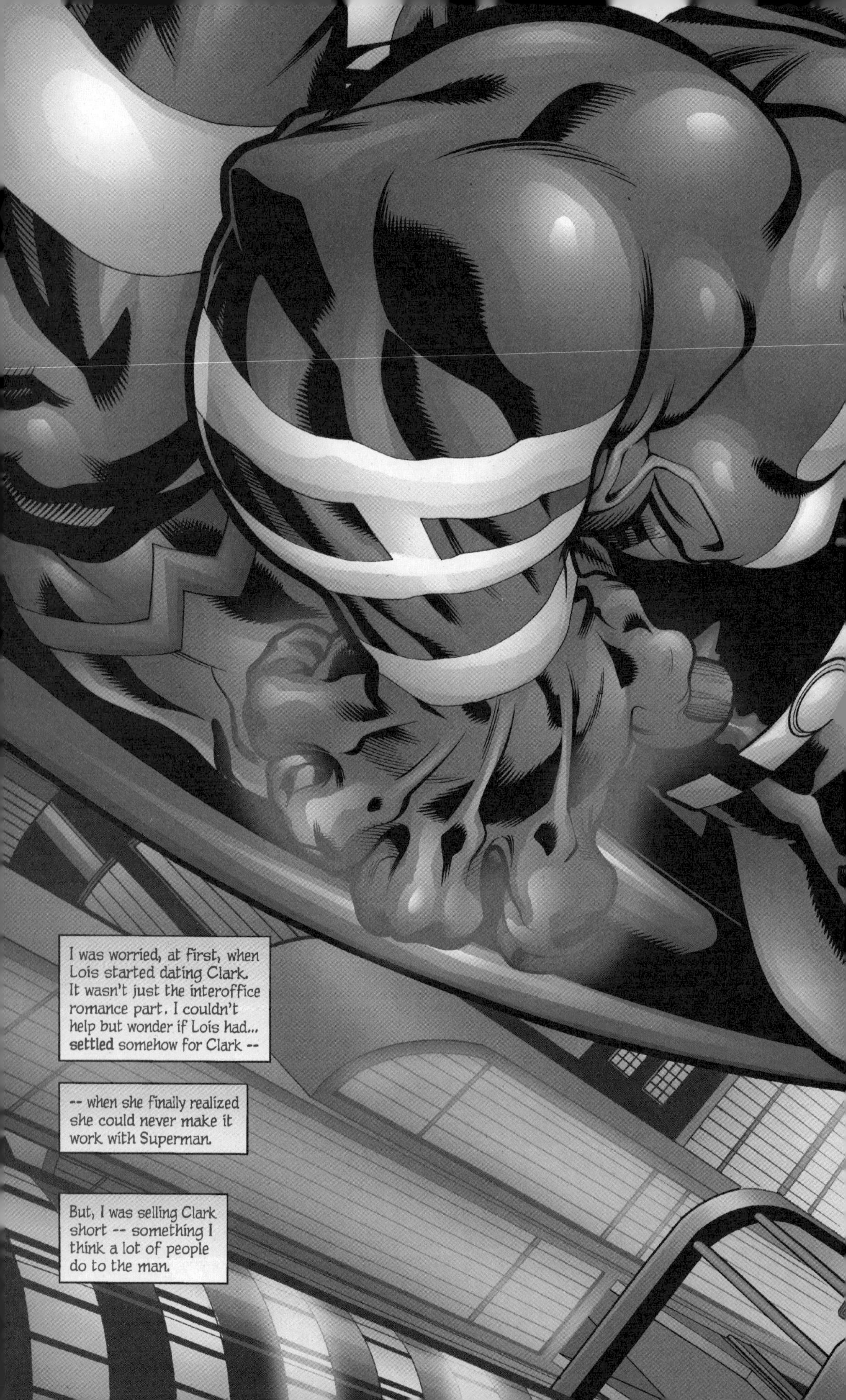
I was worried, at first, when Lois started dating Clark. It wasn't just the interoffice romance part. I couldn't help but wonder if Lois had... **settled** somehow for Clark --
-- when she finally realized she could never make it work with Superman.
But, I was selling Clark short -- something I think a lot of people do to the man.

Clark rose to the occasion every time for Lois.
She had finally found in him a man who not only wasn't intimidated by who she wanted to be, he could even support her, in ways other men -- particularly her father -- had not.
In some ways, she **did** get a Superman, after all.
THIS IS IT, SUPERMAN! ONLY ONE OF US GETS OUT OF THIS ALIVE!

BDOOM
LUTHOR HIGH
SKREEEEC
I WON'T GO BACK TO S.T.A.R. LABS!
I WON'T LET ANYBODY CAGE ME EVER AGAIN!
EVER SINCE I CAME IN CONTACT WITH STRANGE VISITOR, I CAN DO MORE THAN JUST DRAIN YOU!
I CAN KEEP WHAT I TAKE AND I'M TAKIN' WHAT'S LEFT IN YOU!
RUDY, YOU PICKED A BAD DAY TO DO ANYTHING BUT --
KAFF KAFF KAFF
FWOOOSH
-- BLOW YOU OFF!
HIGH
SCRUMCH
CLARK...?
SEE ACTION COMICS #759 -- ED.

ZZRAK
YARRGH!
COLD ENOUGH UP THERE FOR YOU?
LET ME HEAT THINGS UP FOR YOU, RUDY!
THOOM
BDONK
IT'S "PARASITE"!
AFTER TODAY, YOU AND EVERYBODY ELSE WILL RESPECT ME!
KAFF KAFF KAFF
SNKACT

WONDER WOMAN!
YURK
THAT WOULD BE ME.
BAM

I WARNED YOU ABOUT HIS FRIENDS.
GET OUTTA MY HEAD, DOC!
HAVE TO GET THIS LASSO OFF, BEFORE SHE FINDS OUT THE TRUTH.
NNUUNGH
FWING
OOMPH
S'OKAY, KAFF-KAFF WE GOT WHAT WE CAME FOR...
SHOOM

I think about the ups and downs Alice and I have gone through and I'm no expert on marriage, that's for damn sure.
But, I do know something about laying out a newspaper page.
ANYTHING...?
The articles are like jigsaw puzzle pieces. Some are going to fit and some aren't.
You pick your battles knowing that what ma be important today might not matter much tomorrow.
NO... TOO MUCH LEAD IN THE SEWER LINES BENEATH THE CITY.
WITH HIS SPEED, HE COULD BE ANYWHERE.
J'ONN CONTACTED ME. SAID YOU WANTED TO SEE ME?
I GUESS I OWE YOU ONE.
FOR A CHANGE.
I NEED YOUR HELP WITH LOIS. I THINK IT'S TIME WE TOLD HER WHAT HAPPENED IN
KAFF-KAFF-KAFF
VALHALLA.
J'ONN ALSO TOLD ME YOU WEREN'T FEELING WELL. THE PARASITE--?
I DON'T THINK SO. THIS... COUGHING STARTED BEFORE HE ARRIVED, BUT --
SEE ACTION COMICS #761 -- ED.
SUPERMAN -- !
IS HE OKAY?
OMIGOSH, I'M TALKING TO WONDER WOMAN.
IT'S "DIANA," LANA.
YOU KNOW WHO I AM?
WELL, WELL, WELL...

LOOKS LIKE I DIDN'T GET MY INVITATION TO THE SUPERMAN FAN CLUB MEETING.
I CAME DOWN HERE BECAUSE I HEARD YOU HAD BEEN HURT --
-- BUT, IT SEEMS TO ME, YOU'VE GOT EVERYTHING UNDER CONTROL.
HAVE ANY OTHER GIRLFRIENDS DROPPING BY TODAY?
LOIS... YOU'RE BLOWING THIS WAY OUT OF PROPORTION --
-- LET ME FLY YOU TO SOME PLACE WHERE WE CAN HAVE SOME PRIVACY.
DON'T. TOUCH. ME.
IF YOU'LL JUST LISTEN TO WHAT DIANA AND I HAVE TO SAY --
I HAVE ABSOLUTELY NO INTEREST IN ANYTHING YOU AND DIANA HAVE TO SAY!
WE HAD A GOOD THING, SMALLVILLE.
AND YOU BLEW IT.

What's important to remember is that there's always another edition right behind the one you're working on.
Chances to learn from the mistakes you missed. Opportunities to feel good about choices you made.
I CAN'T IMAGINE WHAT YOU HOPE TO ACCOMPLISH BY COMING HERE AT THIS HOUR OF THE NIGHT.
OH, I THINK YOU HAVE... SOME IDEA.
IF THIS IS SOME SORT OF PLOY TO GET ME TO RELEASE YOU FROM YOUR OBLIGATION TO ME --
-- IT'S ALMOST LAUGHABLE.
IS IT?
HOW DID YOU GET PAST SECURITY...?
WASN'T IT YOU WHO ONCE TOLD ME, "IF YOU WANT SOMETHING BAD ENOUGH..."
SO... WHAT IS IT YOU WANT, LOIS?
I THINK THE QUESTION IS --
I've got a feeling that Lois and Clark will work it all out, much in the same way that a newspaper page does...
-- WHAT IS IT YOU WANT, LEX?

I REMEMBER NOTHING BUT MEMORY ITSELF.
AND LOSS.
AND PAIN.
AND RAGE.
WHO AM I? WHY AM I HERE?
WHY DOES IT HURT SO?
AND WHO CAN I PUNISH...

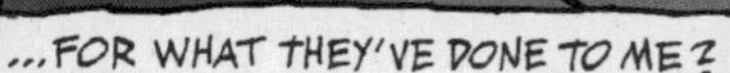

GETTING AWAY FROM IT ALL

J.M. DeMATTEIS writer
PABLO RAIMONDI penciller
JOSE MARZAN, JR. inker
BILL OAKLEY letterer
GLENN WHITMORE & WILDSTORM FX colors
MAUREEN McTIGUE associate editor
EDDIE BERGANZA editor

SUPERMAN created by JERRY SIEGEL & JOE SHUSTER

HOW LONG'S HE GONNA JUST... *FLOAT* THERE, *STEEL* --NOT *SAYING* ANYTHING?

LONG AS HE WANTS, *SUPERGIRL*. LONG AS HE *WANTS*.

C'MON, *S-MAN*-- YOU CALL US ALL HERE... TELL US YOU NEED OUR HELP... SO WHAT'S THE *DEAL?*

I MEAN, FROM THE LOOK ON YOUR FACE, YOU'D THINK IT WAS THE END OF THE *WORLD!*

I'LL BE... UNAVAILABLE... FOR THREE DAYS... MAYBE MORE. I'VE GOT SOMETHING IMPORTANT TO DO--AND NOTHING CAN GET IN THE WAY.
THAT'S WHY I NEED YOU THREE TO KEEP AN EYE ON THINGS FOR ME... ESPECIALLY IN METROPOLIS.
"END OF THE WORLD," SUPERBOY? IN A WAY--
--I GUESS YOU COULD SAY IT IS.
BECAUSE I DON'T CARE WHAT THE CRISIS IS, I'M NOT COMING BACK--
--I CAN'T COME BACK --UNTIL--
UNTIL WHAT?
IT'S... PERSONAL.
SOUNDS LIKE YOU'RE GOING OFF ON A SUICIDE MISSION.
WE'RE YOUR FRIENDS, KAL. YOU CAN TRUST US. I'M SURE THAT WE CAN--
I TOLD YOU, IT'S PERSONAL. IF YOU CAN'T RESPECT THAT--
--I'M SORRY.
I'VE NEVER SEEN HIM LIKE THIS! NEVER! GLOBAL DISASTERS... ALIEN INVASIONS--
--HE'S THE ONE HOLDING IT ALL TOGETHER. HE'S OUR HOPE!
YOU SEE THE LOOK IN HIS EYES? SO COLD. SO--
NO. NOT COLD. HE WAS JUST TRYING TO KEEP IT IN CHECK.
KEEP WHAT IN CHECK?
THAT MAN--

"--IS HURTING."

HI, SWEETIE.
SWEETIE...?
LOIS?
HI.
WHATCHA DOING?
JUST BOMBING AROUND THE INTERNET.
RESEARCH FOR A STORY?
NO.
WELL THEN, WHAT--
LOOK, CLARK-- I'M BUSY HERE. COULD YOU PLEASE STOP BREATHING ALL OVER ME AND--
WHAT?

I JUST CAN'T TAKE THIS ANYMORE! WE'RE LIKE TWO STRANGERS LATELY! I... I DON'T KNOW WHAT TO DO ABOUT YOU ...ABOUT US!
I KNOW THAT YOU'RE UPSET ABOUT ALL THE TIME I'M SPENDING AS SUPERMAN... AND I KNOW LANA♡ SHOWING UP HERE DIDN'T EXACTLY HELP MATTERS MUCH, BUT--
RELAX. ALL MARRIAGES HAVE BUMPY PERIODS. GIVE IT TIME. IT'LL PASS.
♡LAST WEEK IN SUPERMAN #156 --Ed.
LOIS, WE CAN'T JUST SIT AROUND WAITING FOR THINGS TO GET BETTER! WE HAVE TO DO SOMETHING ABOUT IT! WE HAVE TO TAKE ACTION!
RIGHT. MAYBE YOU CAN BUILD A LOIS LANE ROBOT WHO'LL DO EXACTLY WHAT YOU SAY. BETTER YET, YOU CAN USE SUPER-HYPNOSIS TO ENTRANCE ME INTO SUBMISSION--
NOT FUNNY.
EXCUSE ME FOR TRYING TO LIGHTEN THINGS UP A LITTLE.
I... I'VE MADE ARRANGEMENTS FOR US TO GET AWAY TOGETHER FOR A FEW DAYS.
AND I PROMISE YOU THAT SUPERMAN WON'T SPOIL IT.
YEAH, RIGHT.
NO... REALLY! EVERYTHING'S TAKEN CARE OF... NO EMERGENCY'S GOING TO CALL ME AWAY. IT'LL JUST BE YOU AND ME TOGETHER... ALONE.
A CHANCE TO REALLY TALK... TO FIND EACH OTHER AGAIN.
SO WHAT'S IT GONNA BE?
A WEEKEND IN THE WOODS... STUCK IN A SMELLY SLEEPING BAG... WHILE SNAKES CRAWL UP OUR LEGS?
NOT EXACTLY

ANOTHER PLANET?!
YOU'RE TAKING ME TO ANOTHER PLANET?!
I MEAN, IT'S BAD ENOUGH YOU'VE DRAGGED ME HERE TO YOUR LITTLE JLA PLAYHOUSE ON THE MOON, BUT--
IT'LL BE GREAT, LOIS. I PROMISE!
UH... IF YOU TWO WOULD RATHER BE ALONE...?
NO!
I... I'D LIKE YOU TO SHOW ME HOW TO OPERATE THE SHIP, J'ONN. I'M NOT REALLY UP ON MARTIAN TECHNOLOGY.
I THINK I'M GETTING A MIGRAINE.
IT'S THE WATCH-TOWER ATMOSPHERE. IT TAKES A WHILE FOR YOUR BODY TO ACCLIMATE.
KAFF KAFF KAFF
STILL COUGHING?
IT'S NOTHING.
PERHAPS A COOKIE...?
OREOS
I THOUGHT YOU KICKED THAT HABIT?
I CONTROL IT NOW... IT DOES NOT CONTROL ME.
OF COURSE.
NOW ABOUT THE SHIP...?
THE SHIP IS PSIONIC IN NATURE... ADJUSTING ITSELF TO THE PILOT'S PSYCHE.
THE ACTUAL PHYSICAL DEMANDS ARE LIMITED. THE MORE YOU SURRENDER TO THE VESSEL, THE MORE IT WILL SURRENDER TO YOU.
MOST HUMANS WOULD NOT BE ABLE TO FIND THE PSYCHIC BALANCE REQUIRED FOR THE TASK. YOU-- WITH YOUR FORMIDABLE MIND--SHOULD FIND IT CHILD'S PLAY.
WHEN CAN WE GET STARTED?
WHENEVER YOU'D LIKE.

SWELL!
DID HE JUST SAY "SWELL"?
I BELIEVE SO.
:sigh: YOU MIND IF I HAVE ONE OF THOSE?
JUST. ONE.
LET'S HIT THE QUANTUM ROAD, LOIS! WE'VE GOT AN AMAZING JOURNEY AHEAD OF US!
GOODBYE, J'ONN--AND THANKS!
GOOD LUCK, OLD FRIEND.
I THINK YOU'RE GOING TO NEED IT.
MY GOD--
--IT'S BEAUTIFUL!
I BEGAN MY LIFE IN A SHIP NOT ALL THAT DIFFERENT FROM THIS ONE... ROCKETING THROUGH SPACE TOWARD EARTH--
--TOWARD YOU, LOIS.
AND NO MATTER HOW MANY TIMES I'VE TRAVELLED TO THE STARS, IT NEVER FAILS TO MOVE ME. IT TOUCHES SOMETHING IN ME SO DEEP, SO SACRED, THAT--
BOY--YOU REALLY KNOW HOW TO RUIN A MOMENT--!
SORRY.

FOR A FLEETING MOMENT-- I REMEMBER JOY.
I THINK... PERHAPS ...I WAS HAPPY ONCE.
OR IS THAT JUST A WISH? A DREAM?
A LIE CREATED BY A TORTURED MIND?
LIE OR NOT, I ACCEPT IT, I EMBRACE IT.
I BURN.
AND ALL THE MEMORY--ALL DREAMS AND WISHES-- BURN WITH ME.
THE ONLY THING I KNOW NOW, THE ONLY THING I REMEMBER, IS PAIN.
AND ALL I WANT...

...IS TO BE FREE OF IT.
WHO THE HELL DO YOU THINK YOU ARE?!
CONTRARY TO YOUR DELUSIONS, LUTHOR-- YOU DON'T OWN THIS CITY--
--AND YOU DON'T OWN US!
FOR YOU TO DEMAND SUCH MASSIVE PAYMENTS FOR THE USE OF TECHNOLOGY THAT SHOULD BE FREE TO EVERY CITIZEN OF METROPOLIS--
--IT'S OUTRAGEOUS!
AS THE MAYOR OF THIS CITY, I DEMAND THAT ALL DATA RELATING TO THE ALIEN TECHNOLOGY BE IMMEDIATELY TURNED OVER TO ME!
I'VE ASSEMBLED A COALITION OF THE MOST POWERFUL BUSINESSMEN AND POLITICIANS IN METROPOLIS--
--AND I SWEAR TO YOU--
--WE WILL NOT BE HELD HOSTAGE!
LET ME DEAL WITH HIM, OWEN.
YOU KNOW ME, LUTHOR. EDWARD ZEVON.
I OWN HALF THE REAL ESTATE IN THIS CITY, YOU ARROGANT TIN GOD--
--AND I'VE GOT THE POWER AND THE MONEY TO TEAR YOU DOWN OFF THAT PEDESTAL AND--
HOPE...? MERCY...?
KOOM
RAKKKK
I'M SO GLAD YOU'VE ALL HAD A CHANCE TO VENT YOUR FEELINGS... AND AT LEAST PRETEND, FOR A MOMENT, THAT YOU'RE OF ANY CONSEQUENCE.
BUT NOW IT'S TIME TO HAVE DONE WITH YOUR DELUSIONS AND EMBRACE REALITY. AND THE REALITY IS--
THIS --IS MY CITY.

WHATEVER METROPOLIS IS TODAY IS BECAUSE OF MY EFFORTS AND THE EFFORTS OF MY FOREBEARS. EVERY PERSON IN THIS ROOM OWES HIS OR HER SUCCESS TO ME--
--THOUGH MOST OF YOU WOULD BE HARD-PRESSED TO ADMIT IT.
BUT IF YOU SINCERELY BELIEVE THAT YOU CAN DO A BETTER JOB WITH MY CITY THAN I CAN ...SO BE IT.
PERHAPS GOTHAM WOULD BE MORE APPRECIATIVE OF LEXCORP. GOD KNOWS THEY COULD USE THE ECONOMIC BOOST. AND THE TECHNOLOGY.
MY VISION COULD BE EASILY TRANSFERRED TO ANOTHER CITY. NEW YORK, SAN FRANCISCO... IT DOESN'T MATTER.
NO-- THAT'S A LIE. IT DOES MATTER.
FOR THERE IS NO PLACE ON EARTH LIKE METROPOLIS. SHE IS A GEM SHINING IN A DUNGHEAP. I LOVE THIS CITY IN WAYS NONE OF YOU EVER COULD.
BUT I WILL LEAVE--
--AND WHEN I DO--
--BE ASSURED, LADIES AND GENTLEMEN--YOU'LL ALL BE LEAVING WITH ME--
--ONE WAY OR ANOTHER.
UH... LUTHOR. MR. LUTHOR... ON BEHALF OF THE GROUP, I... I'D--
APOLOGY ACCEPTED.
...THERE IT IS, LOIS!
SANCTUS TWELVE!
I'VE ALWAYS WANTED TO COME HERE... IT'S SUPPOSED TO BE ONE OF THE MOST EXTRAORDINARY PLANETS IN EXISTENCE. AN UNTOUCHED, UNSPOILED EDEN.
OH, REALLY? AND WHERE'D YOU HEAR ABOUT THIS ALLEGED PARADISE?
FROM HAL JORDAN.
HAL WHO?
YOU KNOW--THE ORIGINAL GREEN LANTERN.
RIGHT. HAL JORDAN. IT'S HARD FOR ME TO KEEP UP WITH ALL OF YOUR--
--FRIENDS.
HOLY--!
EXACTLY, LOIS.

IT'S... ABSOLUTELY BEAUTIFUL.
BUT IT DOESN'T CHANGE ANYTHING.
...THAT ECHOES MY OWN.
PERHAPS, WITH TIME--
--IT WILL.

EXACTLY.
SOMETHING... HAS CHANGED.
SOMETHING RIPPLES DOWN ...THROUGH MY CONSCIOUS-NESS. A PAIN...
IVING EATURES HEY MOVE OMEWHERE OVE ME.
AND THE IME HERE--
--IS A LITTLE DIFFERENT THAN WE'RE USED TO.
IN THE COURSE OF WHAT WE WOULD CALL A SINGLE DAY, THIS PLANET PASSES THROUGH FOUR.
JUST A FEW DAYS ON SANCTUS--
--CAN GIVE US WEEKS TOGETHER.
SWELL.
THEY WALK A WORLD... I NEVER FORGOT... YET HAVE FAILED TO REMEMBER.

WHY? WHY WAS THE MEMORY OF THAT PLACE TAKEN FROM ME?
REMEMBER WHEN WE WERE FIRST DATING-- AND YOU TOOK ME TO THE METROPOLIS BOTANICAL GARDENS?
...
WELL, IT WAS ONE OF THE MOST WONDER-FUL DAYS WE EVER HAD TOGETHER. IT--
IT WAS A LONG TIME AGO.
WHO CAST ME OUT OF PARADISE...
...AND CONSIGNED ME TO THIS HELL?
OH, LOIS-- FEEL THE SANCTITY ...THE DIVINITY THESE BEINGS RADIATE! IT'S HUMBLING, ISN'T IT? IT'S--
DON'T YOU THINK YOU'RE PROJECTING A LITTLE? THESE AREN'T SOME DANCING SPRITES OUT OF "FANTASIA"--
--THEY'RE ALIEN MONSTERS--
--WHO'D PROBABLY BE THRILLED TO EAT US BOTH FOR DINNER!
WAS IT THEM?
JUST... JUST TELL ME WHAT YOU WANT... WHAT YOU NEED!
I'M SUPERMAN! I CAN GIVE YOU ANYTHING!
THERE IS ONE THING I WANT.
ANYTHING!

I'VE TOLD YOU BEFORE--
--I WANT TO BE LEFT ALONE.
I DON'T UNDERSTAND!
WHAT HAVE I DONE? HAS IT REALLY BEEN SO TERRIBLE BEING MARRIED TO ME?
BLAST IT, LOIS--
WHAT IS THE MATTER WITH YOU?!
JUST... JUST STAY BACK--!
MY GOD--YOU DON'T THINK I'D EVER--
I-I DON'T KNOW WHAT TO THINK...
I'LL BE BACK IN A LITTLE WHILE. AND THEN, IF YOU WANT--
--WE CAN GO HOME.
YES... IT MUST BE THEM! IT HAS TO BE!

I FEEL THE RAGE IN THEIR SOULS... THE SPITE. AND THE FRAGILE LOVE THAT THEIR HEARTS ARE SLOWLY MURDERING.
DEVILS! THEY'VE STOLEN PARADISE FROM ME-- AND THEY DEFILE IT... THEY POISON IT! AND IT'S TIME, AT LONG LAST, FOR ME TO--
TAKE
IT
BACK.

KRA-KOOOM
LOIS!
I-IT JUST CAME BURSTING UP OUT OF THE GROUND--SHRIEKING LIKE A BANSHEE!
IF I HADN'T RUN IT WOULD HAVE KILLED ME! IT WOULD HAVE--
KEEP
AWAY
FROM
MY
WIFE!
CHTHOOM

uh... CLARK--?
DON'T WORRY--
--I'LL NEVER LET YOU FALL!
SO MUCH FOR YOUR PURE AND PERFECT EDEN! WHAT IS THAT MONSTROSITY?
RRUMBLLE
I'M NOT SURE-- BUT, AS IT TOUCHED ME, I COULD ACTUALLY FEEL THE HEAT FROM THE THING... BURNING MY FLESH!
NO, NOT JUST MY FLESH, LOIS-- IT WAS PERMEATING MY MIND... MY SOUL!
BUT THERE WAS SOMETHING ELSE-- SOMETHING ALMOST INDEFINABLE! AS IF THE CREATURE WAS TRYING--
--TO--
THOOM

BROOMFF
OUCH.
THIS IS NOT--
kaff kaff kaff
--WORKING OUT THE WAY I--
--EXPECTED--!
OH!
NOW I GET IT!

...HANG ON, LOIS! I'M HERE-- AND I'VE BROUGHT THE CAVALRY!
MY GOD, LOIS--ARE YOU ALL RIGHT?
WHAT HAPPENED HERE?!
THE MONSTER... CAME RUSHING TOWARD ME... LIKE IT WAS GOING TO KILL ME... AND THEN-- THEN IT JUST--OH, CLARK, IT WAS AWFUL--
IT JUST SCREAMED AND... EXPLODED! IMPLODED! I DON'T KNOW!
THESE BEINGS--THE Z'TORRI --THEY'RE EVERYTHING I THOUGHT THEY WERE--
--AND THEY COMMUNICATE IN AN EXTRAORDINARY WAY! NOT THROUGH WORDS...OR TELEPATHY... BUT THROUGH WAVES OF PALPABLE FEELINGS THAT--
THEN--IT NEVER HAD A CHANCE.
"A CHANCE"? WHAT DO YOU MEAN?
IT WAS NO MONSTER. IT WAS ONE OF THEIR YOUNG.
WHEN THE Z'TORRI REACH WHAT WE WOULD CALL PUBERTY... WHICH FOR THEM COMES AFTER SEVERAL HUNDRED YEARS--
--THEY DESCEND INTO THE BOWELS OF THE PLANET-- COCOON THEMSELVES--
--AND, OVER THE COURSE OF DECADES, BURN OFF THE IMPURITIES IN THEIR SOULS. FEAR, RAGE, SELFISHNESS--
--ANYTHING THAT COMES BETWEEN THEIR INDIVIDUAL EGO-MINDS AND COMMUNION WITH THEIR RACE, THEIR WORLD--
--THE UNIVERSE ITSELF.
BUT IT'S NOT A GENTLE TRANSFORMATION. ALL THEIR DARKEST FEELINGS ARE BOILED TO THE SURFACE--
SOMEHOW, OUR PRESENCE ON THE PLANET DISTURBED THE PROCESS--AND DROVE THE YOUNG ONE UP, OUT OF ITS COCOON--
--TOO--
--SOON...?!

CLARK--IS IT THE SAME CREATURE THAT--?
YES.
AND IT'S--COMMUNICATING WITH YOU?
THE Z'TORRI SAYS THAT... WHEN I TOUCHED IT... THE LOVE IN MY HEART--THE LOVE I FEEL FOR YOU, LOIS--
--WAS ENOUGH TO IGNITE THE FADING SPARK OF LIFE... AND ALLOW IT TO COMPLETE ITS RE-BIRTHING PROCESS.
AND --IS IT SAYING ANYTHING--
--ELSE?
WAIT! DON'T GO!

HA HA HA HA HA
WHAT'S THE JOKE?
DON'T YOU SEE? IT'S AS IF THIS ENCOUNTER... WAS FATED TO BE! THAT POOR BEING STRUGGLED... SUFFERED... JUST AS WE'VE BEEN SUFFERING--
--BUT IN THE END... LOVE... OUR LOVE--WAS ENOUGH TO--
"LOVE CONQUERS ALL"? IT'S A NICE FAIRY TALE, CLARK. BUT LIFE'S NOT THAT SIMPLE.
I WISH IT WAS.
BUT--
TAKE ME HOME, CLARK.
NOW.
SURE, LOIS--
WHATEVER YOU WANT.

THE BEGINNING IS A FRIGHTENING TIME.
¡KOFF, KOFF¡

I--UM--I NEED TO BE GONE FOR AWHILE, LOIS...
...BUSINESS...
¡KOFF¡

WHATEVER. DON'T LET THE DOOR HIT YOUR CAPE ON THE WAY OUT.
AND CAN'T YOU HAVE KELEX CHECK OUT THAT WRETCHED COUGH?
...WATCH ME PULL A RABBIT OUTTA...

...MY HAT. NOTHIN' UP MY SLEEVE...
UH, OH. LOOK AT THE TIME, NATASHA. DUTY CALLS...
HEH, HEH...

GUY, UNC! THE NEXT EPISODE IS A CLASSIC!
I KNOW, I KNOW--BUT TIME WAITS FOR NO SUPERMAN.
NOW YOU REMEMBER THE DRILL. WE'LL BE BACK BY MORNING AND I NEED YOU TO HAVE THE STEELWORKS UP AND RUNNING...

THE BEGINNING IS ALWAYS A FRIGHTENING TIME. IN THE CRUCIBLE OF CREATION, CHAOS RULES--THE UNKNOWN AND THE TERRIBLE HAUNT AND PREY UPON A DISORIENTED MANKIND. FORCES THAT CAN NOT BE BE CONTROLLED STALK THE LAND.
...SO WHEN THE CTESSON PARTICLES GENERATED BY OUR HEMICLOUD CHAMBER EXCITE THE PROBABILITY FIELD ASSOCIATED WITH THE TRACE SINGULARITY...
...THE RESULTING POLARITY REVERSAL SHOULD SLIDE THE GHOST DOWN INTO OUR PLASMA TRAP.
UNDERSTAND?
IN THE BEGINNING, A VULNERABLE MANKIND MUST LOOK TO ITS HEROES. THE NAVAJO TURNED TO THEIR TWIN WAR-GODS TO PROTECT THEIR BELEAGUERED HOME FROM MONSTERS AND ALIEN GODS.
NO.
THAT'S WHY I ASKED FOR YOUR HELP.
BUT IT'S VERY SIMPLE IF YOU JUST VISUALIZE THE QUANTUM GRID IN TERMS OF A 4-DIMENSIONAL NEO-PLANCK EQUATION...
...THE PROTO-GREEKS SURVIVED THANKS TO THE BROTHER TITANS PROMETHEUS AND EPIMETHEUS, WHO DELIVERED POWER, AND FIRE, AND HOPE TO MANKIND...
STEEL--I DON'T KNOW THAT I'M EVER GOING TO COMPREHEND THE WHY BEHIND ALL OF THIS...
I'M JUST GLAD IT STILL EXISTS--AND CAN BE RETRIEVED.
OH, WE CAN DO MORE THAN JUST RETRIEVE IT...
...AND THE ANCIENT KRYPTONIAN BOLMETH PEOPLE CREDIT THEIR GOLDEN AGE TO A BENEVOLENT COLLABORATION BETWEEN YLA-UTH, THE SUN-LORD AND KOR-OP, THE EARTH-GIANT.
...ONCE THE TRACE SINGULARITY HAS BEEN CAPTURED IN THE SPECTRAL NEXUS APPARATUS' STABILIZATION CHAMBER...
DIFFERENT TIMES, DIFFERENT WORLDS, DIFFERENT CULTURES-- BUT THE STORY ALWAYS REMAINS THE SAME. THE BEGINNING IS A DELICATE THING, AND SO MUCH CAN GO WRONG...

Creation Story
MARK SCHULTZ writer
DOUG MAHNKE penciller
TOM NGUYEN inker
KEN LOPEZ letterer
GLENN WHITMORE WILDSTORM FX colors
MAUREEN McTIGUE associate editor
EDDIE BERGANZA editor
Special Thanks to LOUISE SIMONSON & JON BOGDANOVE for getting us here & JOEL MOEN, PAT GLEASON, GORDON PURCELL and SHAWN MOLL!
...ONCE THE GHOST IS IN THE BOTTLE...
...WE'RE CARTING IT BACK TO METROPOLIS AND BUILDING YOU THE BEST FORTRESS OF SOLITUDE A SUPERMAN EVER HAD!
SUPERMAN created by JERRY SIEGEL and JOE SHUSTER

KELEX CALLED IT A GHOST FORTRESS BECAUSE HE SAID IT WAS LIKE THE SOUL OF A MAN WHO COULDN'T ACCEPT HIS OWN DEATH, JOHN.
NOT A BAD ANALOGY. THE INCREDIBLE POWER RELEASED WITH THE STRIKE OF LUTHOR'S KRYPTONITE MISSILE--
--SHOCKED THE ANNIHILATED MATERIAL BODY OF THE FORTRESS INTO PERMANENTLY HOLDING TO WHAT SHOULD HAVE BEEN A TRANSITORY STATE ON ITS WAY TO PURE, RELEASED ENERGY...
KOFF
...AND THUS, ALLOWING US TO NOW COLLECT THE ATOMIC MEMORY OF EVERYTHING THAT EVER EXISTED IN THE FORTRESS.
WISH YOU'D HAVE KELEX CHECK THAT COUGH.
I'M ALL RIGHT.
KOFF
IN THE BEGINNING, THE NEW WORLD GROWS FROM THE ASHES OF THE OLD. BUT EVEN AS LAW, LOGIC AND ORDER TAKE FORM, THE AGENTS OF ANARCHY, OF UNBRIDLED CREATION, REMAIN UNDETERRED.
...THEY ARE CALLED TRICKSTER--COYOTE--UTGARD-LOKI...
010111101001 011110001010 101001010100 10100...

...THEY ARE THE FOOT SOLDIERS OF CHAOS.
...0101111010010 1111000101010100 101010010100...
OUR WEEKS OF OF INFILTRATION AND METICULOUS OBSERVATION WILL FINALLY PAY OFF, LUNA...
OF COURSE. THERE WAS NEVER A DOUBT.
EXCELLENT.
VERY GOOD. POLYPHEMUS 212 REPORTS THAT THE CAPTURE WAS SUCCESSFUL.
IN ADDITION TO THE BRAINIAC 13 TECHNOLOGY WE CONTINUE TO UNLOCK, WE'LL SOON POSSESS THE SECRETS OF KRYPTONIAN SCIENCE.
WE MOVE CLOSER, CYBERMOTHS! CLOSER TO THE DAY WHEN WE SEIZE METROPOLIS!
ALL HAIL LUNA, QUEEN OF THE CYBERNETIC UNDERGROUND!
ALL HAIL ME, YOU BET.
IS IT READY, SPHINX 44? AM I SET TO SPEAK WITH HE WHO CALLS THE SHOTS?
THE OVERMIND IS WAITING, LUNA...

"...CRYPTO-MODEM ENGAGED!"
HE WHO CALLS THE SHOTS??
A POOR ATTEMPT AT HUMOR, OBSCURE ONE.
THE TENSION HERE IS THICK ENOUGH TO CUT.

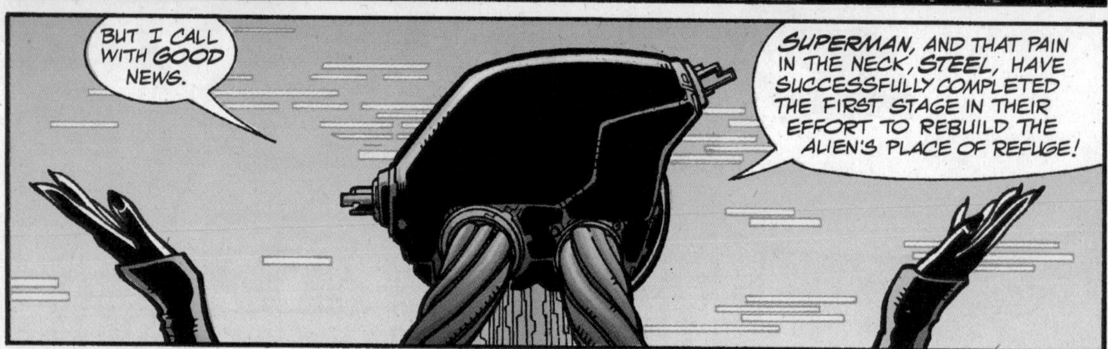
BUT I CALL WITH GOOD NEWS.
SUPERMAN, AND THAT PAIN IN THE NECK, STEEL, HAVE SUCCESSFULLY COMPLETED THE FIRST STAGE IN THEIR EFFORT TO REBUILD THE ALIEN'S PLACE OF REFUGE!

I SEE.
AND YOU WERE PLANNING TO BRING ME UP TO DATE ON THE COURSE OF OUR OPERATION IN THAT ARENA? OR MUST I...
UNCLENCH YOUR OVERBROW, MY OVERMIND. APOLOGIES FOR MY NEGLIGENCE.
ALLOW ME TO BRING YOU UP TO SPEED...

...TWO WEEKS AGO, AGENT GYPSY 84 MANAGED TO GAIN ACCESS TO THE ANNOYING STEEL'S LABORATORIES--
--WHERE, INCREDIBLY ENOUGH, HE WITNESSED OUR ANTAGONIST MIDWIFING THE BIRTH OF A TESSERACT--

"CONTINUING TO OVERRIDE THE STEELWORKS' 813 TRANSMODED SECURITY SYSTEMS, GYPSY 84 LEARNED OF SUPERMAN AND STEEL'S PLANS FOR THIS POCKET DIMENSION...
...INFINITE SPACE WITHIN A FINITE DIMENSIONAL CONTAINMENT! I'VE SEEN THEM IN THE FUTURE.
IF MY FORTRESS COULD BE REBUILT WITHIN THERE-- WOULD THAT BE POSSIBLE?
WELL, THEORETICALLY YES -- BUT...
"...THEY STRUCK A DEAL-- FORMED A PARTNERSHIP...
THIS IS KELEX. HE HOLDS THE FORTRESS' COMPLETE COMPUTER FILES IN HIS MEMORY.
MY KNOWLEDGE OF KRYPTONIAN SCIENCE COUPLED WITH YOUR ENGINEERING SKILLS CAN MAKE THIS HAPPEN, MASTER IRONS.
WHILE WHO PAYS THE BILLS?
"...AND BEGAN ACTUALIZING THE CONTROLLED REBIRTH OF KRYPTONIAN TECHNOLOGY ON EARTH.
IT'S A SOLITON-GENERATOR-- IT ALLOWED ME TO ESCAPE THE PHANTOM ZONE.
I SUPPOSE ITS FUNCTION COULD BE RECONFIGURED INTO THAT OF AN INTER-DIMENSIONAL PORTAL.
EXCUSE ME, MISTRESS NATASHA, BUT THE MASTERS WILL BE NEEDING ME...
THE MASTERS, HUH? SOMEONE NEEDS THEIR SOCIAL AWARENESS RESPONSE RECALIBRATED.

"WHILE STEEL AND THE ROBOT BRAINSTORMED THE SCIENCE OF RECONSTRUCTION, SUPERMAN WOULD DISAPPEAR REPEATEDLY TO WHO KNOWS WHERE...
TO REMATERIALIZE THE FORTRESS, JOHN HENRY SAYS WE'LL NEED TONS OF RAW MATERIALS...
...THE COPPER LEFT IN THIS ABANDONED MINE WILL BE A START.
KRUMPF
KRUNCH
"...RETURNING WITH HUGE QUANTITIES OF THE STUFF FROM WHICH THE GHOST FORTRESS WILL DRAW MOLECULAR SUBSTANCE.
NATASHA! WHAT ARE YOU...?
OH, JUST MAKING A MINOR RESPONSE ALTERATION.
IT'LL MAKE FOR A MORE WELL-ADJUSTED SUPPORT TEAM-- RIGHT, KELEX?
SPRRRK
"THEY HAVE WORKED NONSTOP ON THIS PROJECT, CHALLENGING OUR ABILITY TO KEEP PACE."
THE QUANTUM RADICAL GOVERNOR WILL NEED ADJUSTMENTS, KELEX.
WILL DO.
THE GIFFLER WRENCH, BIG BLUE. SHAKE A LEG.

"ONLY OUR EFFORTS TO TAP AND DECRYPT THE B13 TECHNOLOGY--SOMETHING STEEL AND SUPERMAN HAVE NOT HAD THE TIME TO DO--HAVE ALLOWED US TO CONTINUE OUR SECRET OBSERVATIONS.
IT'S LIKE A CHINESE PUZZLE. THE FORTRESS WILL LIE WITHIN THE TESSERACT, WHICH WILL BE KEPT IN THIS CONTAINMENT SPHERE.
THE SPHERE MUST BE RECONFIGURED AND PROPERLY ALIGNED BEFORE IT WILL OPEN. ONLY A MAN OF YOUR STRENGTH CAN HANDLE IT.
ONE THING I'VE LEARNED IS THAT THERE'S NEVER TOO MUCH SECURITY.
I CALL IT THE SPECTRAL NEXUS APPARATUS. IT'S GOING TO BRING YOUR GHOST FORTRESS TO THE TESSERACT.
I CALL IT THE SPECNAP. SO DOES KELEX.
I GUESS WE'RE READY TO GO.
KOFF
"WHICH BRINGS ME TO LEXCORP. HOW HE DOES IT, I DON'T KNOW, BUT LUTHOR HAS MANAGED TO KEEP US CHOKING IN THE DUST, WELL BEHIND HIS UNDERSTANDING AND MASTERY OF THE GIFTS LEFT BY BRAINIAC 13...
"...IF WE ARE TO CHALLENGE HIM FOR CONTROL OF THIS NEW METROPOLIS, WE NEED AN OUTSIDE ADVANTAGE.
"WITH THAT IN MIND, I FORMULATED A PLAN. POLYPHEMUS Z12 WOULD INTEGRATE HIMSELF WITH THE SPECNAP AND..."

I HAVE BEEN IN CONTACT WITH A DISTANT-OTHER.
ENOUGH. WE'VE ALREADY DISCUSSED YOUR PLAN.
HE IS EAGER TO BE FREE TO AVENGE HIMSELF ON SUPERMAN, BUT BE AWARE...

...HIS WINDOW OF OPPORTUNITY IS VERY NARROW, AND SO YOUR TIMING MUST BE PRECISE.
NOW GO! BRING ME THIS TECHNOLOGY THAT WILL DELIVER METROPOLIS FROM LUTHOR'S HANDS...

...AND INTO OURS!
SO BE IT, YOUR OVERMINDEDNESS! IT'S SHOW TIME!
CYBERMOTHS! WHAT IS TRUE POWER?

KNOWLEDGE IS TRUE POWER!!
THEY THAT CONTROL THE INFORMATION STREAM HOLD THE HIGH GROUND!!

BEWARE THE TRICKSTER-- HE IS A SHAPE-SHIFTER.
SO I STILL DON'T UNDERSTAND WHY YOU DIDN'T JUST GO TO THE JLA WITH THE PROJECT...
JOHN HENRY, THE JLA IS FINE IN ITS PLACE--BUT IT--CAN BE *KOFF*--
--I NEED SOMEONE CLOSE WHO CAN MONITOR METROPOLIS WHEN I'M CALLED AWAY.

YOU'RE GOOD AT WHAT YOU DO.
I KNOW I CAN TRUST YOU TO BE DISCREET WITH KRYPTONIAN SECRETS, AND I THOUGHT THE STEELWORKS COULD BECOME A SORT OF LOCAL SUBSTATION OF THE FORTRESS...
WELL, FAR BE IT FROM ME TO SAY NO TO AN INFUSION OF KRYPTONIAN SCIENCE. SHOULD HELP GET THE B13 BUGS UNDER CONTROL.

...INITIATE TOTAL INTEGRATION PROCESS, POLYPHEMUS 212-- REPEAT...

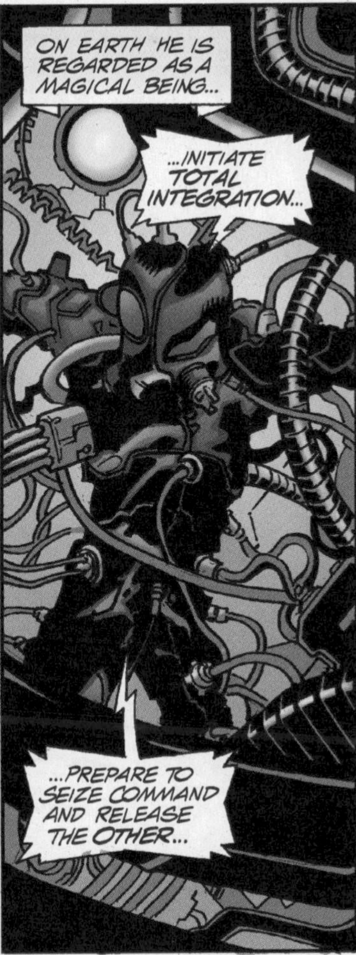
ON EARTH HE IS REGARDED AS A MAGICAL BEING...
...INITIATE TOTAL INTEGRATION...
...PREPARE TO SEIZE COMMAND AND RELEASE THE OTHER...

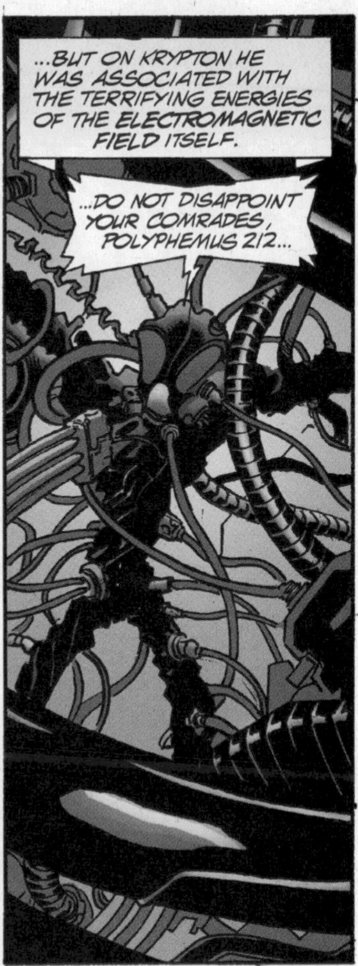
...BUT ON KRYPTON HE WAS ASSOCIATED WITH THE TERRIFYING ENERGIES OF THE ELECTROMAGNETIC FIELD ITSELF.
...DO NOT DISAPPOINT YOUR COMRADES, POLYPHEMUS 212...

BY SHIFTING TO IMITATE THE FAMILIAR, BY MELDING WITH THE TRUSTED, THE TRICKSTER GUARANTEES HIS WELCOME TO HEARTH AND HOME.
HEADS UP, NAT! WE'RE BACK!
HOW WAS YOUR "CLASSIC EPISODE"?
EVEN FUNNIER THAN THE LAST TIME I SAW IT.
BUT NOT AS DEEPLY MEANINGFUL WITHOUT YOU THERE.
WE'RE READY TO RUMBLE, OH, AUTHORITY FIGURES...
...ALL FIRED UP AND THE POT'S ON THE STOVE.
PLEASE MOVE YOUR BUTT, BIG BLUE.
THEN LET'S GET THIS SHOW ON THE ROAD!
OPEN THE CONTAINMENT SPHERE--ACCESS THE TESSERACT!

HURRY! THE SOONER WE GET THE GHOST FORTRESS PROJECTED, THE BETTER.
LIKE WE PRACTICED--BOTH OF YOU WILL GO INSIDE.
THE REVERSED SPECNAP WILL DISGORGE THE GHOST FORTRESS INTO THE TESSERACT...
...AND CARRY YOU ALONG WITH IT.
ONCE INSIDE, IT'S UP TO YOU TO ACTIVATE OUR CONSTRUCTION PROGRAM!
NATASHA--LET 'ER RIP!
IT WORKED, KELEX!
WE'RE BACK IN THE GHOST FORTRESS!
FRESH.

THEY'RE IN!
BUT-- THIS IS STRANGE--
--I'M GETTING SOME EXOTIC READINGS...

TASHA-- DO A VISUAL INSPECTION OF THE SPECNAP...
A VISUAL INSPECTION? CHEEEEEZ!
TASH...

OKAY, OKAY.
LIKE I'M REALLY GOING TO FIND ANYTHING...
...LIKE, WHILE YOU WERE FLYING IT HERE, YOU MIGHT HAVE DROPPED IT OR SOMETHING...

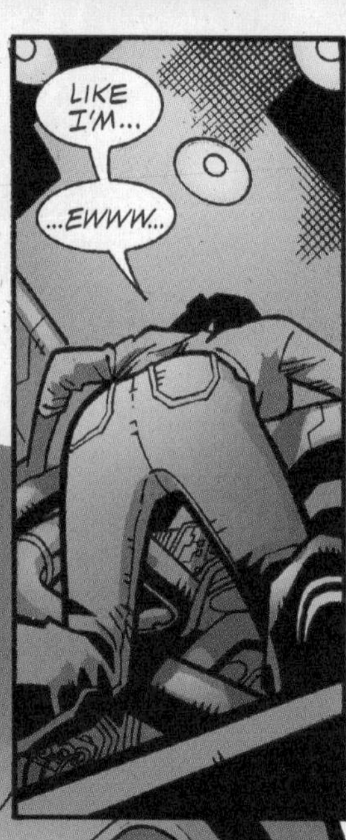
LIKE I'M...
...EWWW...

UNC...?

THAT-- IS NOT GOOD...
...GOT TO ALERT SUPER...
I THINK NOT, DR. IRONS...

I THINK EVERYTHING IS JUST FINE AS IS.
AND SO THE TRICKSTER PREPARES THE WAY FOR THE ADVENT OF CHAOS.
THE MOTHS?!
THE CYBERMOTHS.
AND I AM LUNA, YOUR OFFICIAL CYBERMOTH REPRESENTATIVE.
YOU'VE BEEN QUITE THE THORN IN OUR SIDE, DR. IRONS, WHAT WITH YOUR HABITUAL DISRUPTIONS OF OUR DIGITAL SIPHONING OPERATIONS...
...BUT NOW I THINK YOUR SCIENTIFIC PROWESS WILL DO US SOME GOOD.
PLEASE DON'T GO TRYING ANYTHING HEROIC--YOU MAY BE BULLETPROOF IN THAT ARMOR, BUT I DOUBT YOUR NIECE IS.

HOW...?
WHY...?

HOW? THROUGH A SUPERIOR KNOWLEDGE OF THE INFRASTRUCTURE CHANGES WROUGHT BY THE B13 VIRUS.
WE KNOW YOUR SYSTEMS BETTER THAN YOU DO.
WE OWN YOUR SECURITY PROGRAMS.

WHY?
BECAUSE WE CAN.

THAT'S ALL YOU NEED TO KNOW FOR NOW, SCIENCE BOY.
CHAINS, PLEASE...

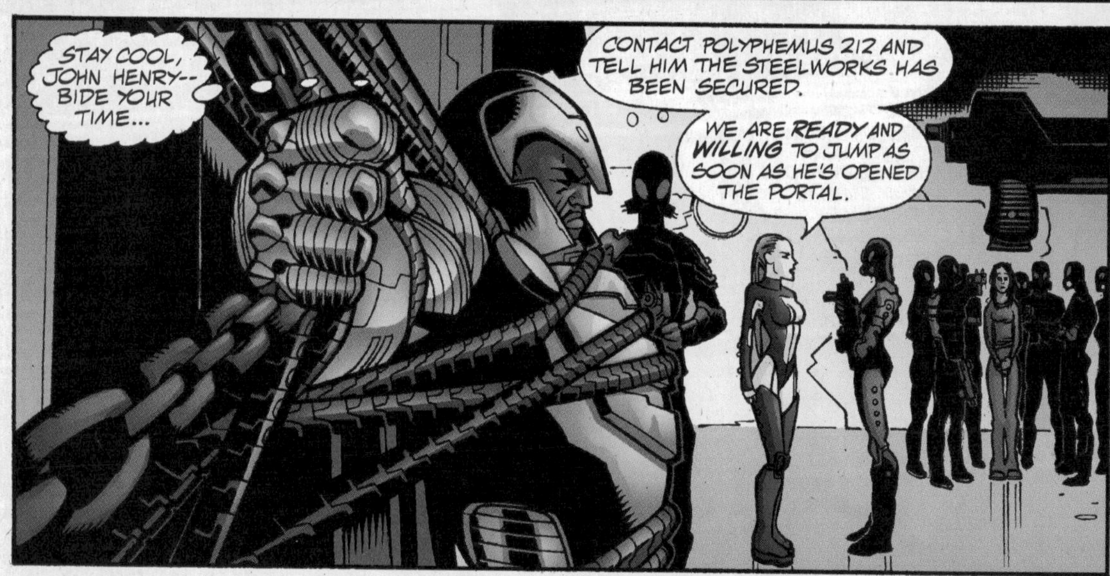
STAY COOL, JOHN HENRY-- BIDE YOUR TIME...
CONTACT POLYPHEMUS 212 AND TELL HIM THE STEELWORKS HAS BEEN SECURED.
WE ARE READY AND WILLING TO JUMP AS SOON AS HE'S OPENED THE PORTAL.

HERE THEY COME, KELEX-- RIGHT ON SCHEDULE...
...THE "GHOSTS" OF ROBOT SECURITY...
...ATTACKING LIKE ANTIBODIES ON A MICROBE.
BRRRR! CONTACT DOESN'T FEEL ANY BETTER NOW THAN IT DID ON OUR FIRST TRIP INTO THIS NETHERWORLD.
I'D APPRECIATE IT IF YOU'D COMPLETE YOUR PARTICLE LINK A.S.A.P.
IN MAN OF STEEL #90-- ED
CHILL. BLUE.
INTERSTITIAL COMPUTER LINKAGE IS COMING ON LINE.
THE FORTRESS COMPUTERS NOW RECOGNIZE AND ACCEPT US...
...AND I HAVE ENGAGED THE CONSTRUCTION PROGRAM DESIGNED BY UNCLE JOHN AND MY OWN BAD SELF.
OBSERVE--HERE COME THE TONS AND TONS OF RAW MATTER NEEDED TO BUILD THE BONES OF A HEALTHY, GROWING FORTRESS.
KICK IT!

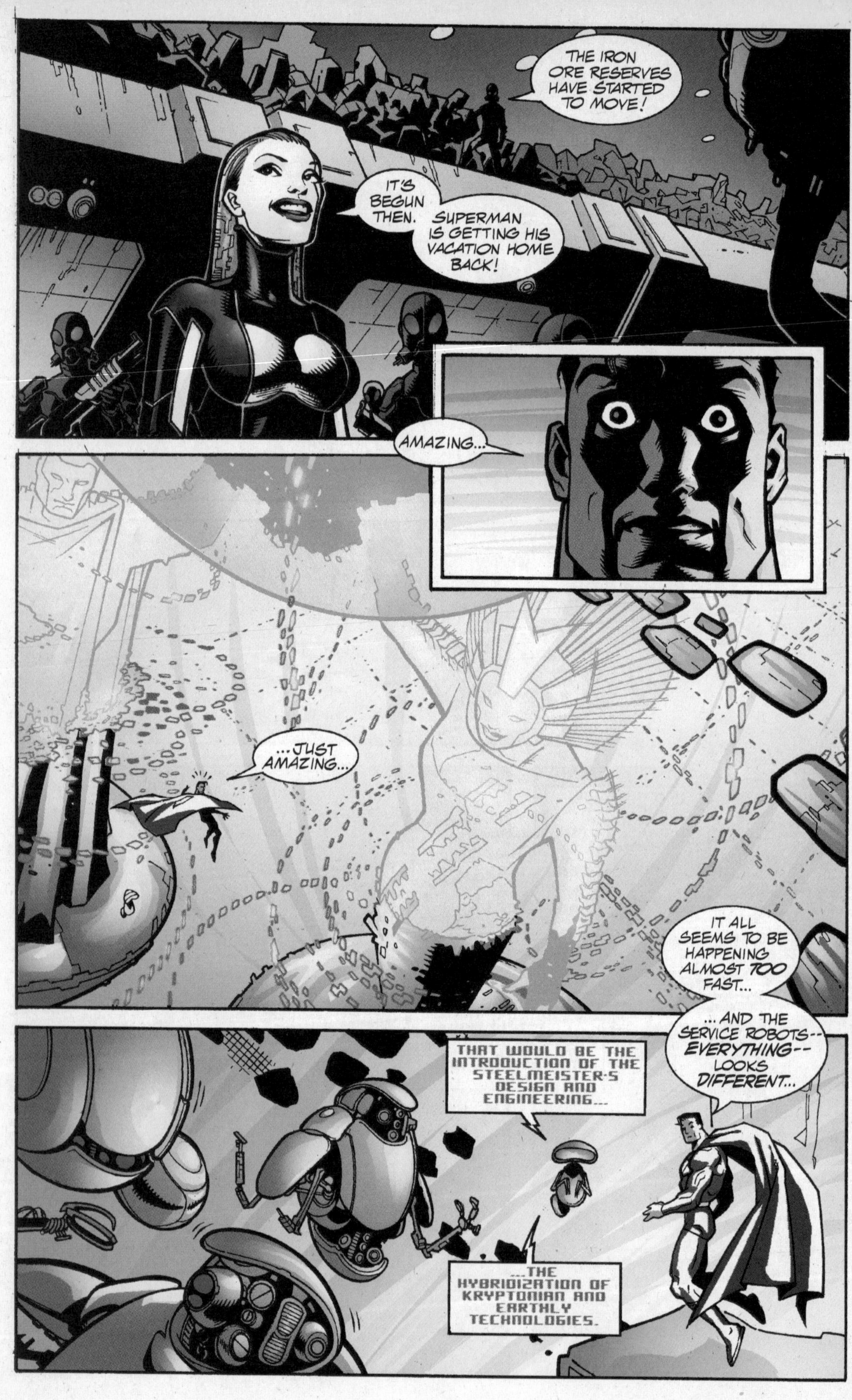
THE IRON ORE RESERVES HAVE STARTED TO MOVE!
IT'S BEGUN THEN.
SUPERMAN IS GETTING HIS VACATION HOME BACK!
AMAZING...
...JUST AMAZING...
IT ALL SEEMS TO BE HAPPENING ALMOST TOO FAST...
...AND THE SERVICE ROBOTS--EVERYTHING--LOOKS DIFFERENT...
THAT WOULD BE THE INTRODUCTION OF THE STEELMEISTER'S DESIGN AND ENGINEERING...
...THE HYBRIDIZATION OF KRYPTONIAN AND EARTHLY TECHNOLOGIES.

"IN ADDITION TO ALL THAT, THE ESTABLISHMENT OF THIS SOLITON-ACTIVATED PORTAL TO THE PHANTOM ZONE SHOULD ALLOW YOU ACCESS, IF NECESSARY, TO THAT FAR PLANE OF EXISTENCE.

"IT'S A RISKY ENDEAVOR, NEVER BEFORE ATTEMPTED...

"...BUT WE'VE BEEN THROUGH THIS ALL BEFORE. YOU BELIEVE THE BENEFITS OUTWEIGH THE RISKS."

"AS FAR AS THE POSSIBILITY OF RECOVERING THE DIMENSIONALLY-CHALLENGED CITY OF KANDOR...
"...ALL EVIDENCE INDICATES IT SURVIVED, BUT ITS RETURN RAISES SO MANY PROBABILITY ISSUES THAT I CAN NOT BEGIN TO HAZARD...
"BIG BLUE...?"
BIG BLUE, ARE YOU, LIKE, ILL?
ARE YOU NOT FUNCTIONING AS PER YOUR NORMAL...
I--I'M OKAY-- ;KOFF;...
...IT'S JUST-- EVERYTHING-- HAPPENING SO FAST...
...I...
WHAT'S THA...?
ALERT! ALERT!

INTRUDER ALERT!
SOMETHING HAS INVADED SYSTEMS!
BUT THEY JUST FORMED! WHAT COULD POSSIBLY...?
MAXIMUM ALERT!
AN ALIEN PRESENCE HAS INFECTED PROGRAMMING AND IS IN CONTROL OF THE PHANTOM ZONE LOCKS!
SENSORS INDICATE POLYPHEMUS 212 IS NOW IN THE PROCESS OF EXPENDING HIS FINAL ENERGIES TO THE RELEASE OF THE OTHER.
REST IN PEACE, COMRADE 212.
GENTLEMEN-- PREPARE FOR IMMEDIATE ACTION!
YOU'RE TOO LATE, SUPERMAN...
TOO LATE TO STOP ME FROM RETURNING...
WHUMM
...TOO LATE TO CLOSE THE DOOR ON MY VENGEANCE!

LOOK AT ME, SUPERMAN!
LOOK AT WHAT YOU'VE DONE TO ME!!
THE CYBORG!
GAKKK!

IT WORKED!
WE'RE IN!

THIS IS INSANE! WHERE DID THIS LUNATIC COME FROM...
...AND WHO ARE THOSE CHARACTERS?
WITH THE STATE OF THE FORTRESS IN FLUX, EVERYTHING MUST BE VULNERABL...
UHHHNN...
ZZRK
I SAID LOOK AT ME, SUPERMAN!!
I WANT THIS TWISTED HORROR THAT I'VE BECOME...
KRUNCH
...TO BE THE LAST VISION THAT EVER CROSSES YOUR TREACHEROUS ALIEN EYES!
SMASH
KNOCK KNOCK

UM--I JUST STOPPED BY TO-- UH--SAY HI TO NATASHA?
I COULD COME BACK IF THIS ISN'T A GOOD TIME...
BORIS!
BORIS..?
OUCH!
BRAAAPP
BRAAAPP
I'M HOME FREE, UNC!
SHOW 'EM YOUR STUFF!
THE RANK AND FILE CYBERMOTH IS APPARENTLY NOT VERY BRIGHT--THEY DIDN'T THINK TO PUT SECURITY BACK UP!
BORIS, I WAS NEVER HAPPIER TO SEE YOU!
BRAAAPP
KKRRRRNNCH
BORIS! NATASHA! YOU KEEP YOUR HEADS DOWN!
AND YOU CREEPY VERMIN...

HEROES FACE THE ADVANCE OF CHAOS AS ONE, THEIR POWERS PERSONIFYING THE TWO WORLDS KNOWN TO THE ANCIENTS.
...DON'T YOU EVER POINT A GUN AT MY NIECE AGAIN!
THE EARTH-GIANT, THE FORGE OF THE GODS, DRAWING HIS STRENGTH FROM THE PLANET ITSELF...
...AND THE SUN-LORD MASTER OF THE SKY, THE BRINGER OF LIFE FROM THE HEAVENS.
KRAK
URRRK!
NOT IMPRESSIVE, SUPERMAN...

HURRY! WE ONLY HAVE *MINUTES* TO SIPHON THE KRYPTONIAN COMPUTER'S ENTIRE MEMORY!

SECURITY SHIELDS MAY COME ON LINE AT ANY TIME, AND THIS BATTLE ISN'T GOING TO LAST FOREVER...

"...ALTHOUGH THE OVERMIND'S WILD CARD PARTNER DOES SEEM TO BE DOING HIS JOB."

LOOK AT WHAT *YOU* CREATED WHEN YOU THREW ME INTO THAT DIMENSIONAL RIFT!

IN ADVENTURES OF SUPERMAN #563 -- ED.

IN THE BEGINNING, THE SUN-LORD SEES HOW WEAK MANKIND IS. HE TAKES PITY AND CRUSADES TO TURN ALL MAN'S ENEMIES TO MONSTERS OF STONE.
THWACK
...I ONLY DID WHAT I HAD TO DO!
ONLY DID WHAT YOU...?
IS THAT THE BEST YOU CAN OFFER?
THIS IS ALMOST DISAPPOINTING!
WHY, LOOK AT YOU!
YOU'RE -- SICKLY...
...DISGUSTING...
BUT HE OFFENDS THE GODS ALONG THE WAY, AND MUST FACE HIS OWN DEATH...
WHAT'S HAPPENED TO YOU? I DREAMED OF TAKING YOU OUT AT THE HEIGHT OF YOUR POWER...
...BUT NOW I COULD JUST SQUASH YOU LIKE A...

...BEFORE WINNING ALLIES THAT AID IN HIS TRIUMPHANT REBIRTH.
AIEEEEE!
ZZZSSSSSSS
WHAT... ...CERIZAH-- OF KANDOR?
JUST RELAX, SUPERMAN...
IT'S OVER, CYBORG. YOU'RE GOING BACK.
HE--HE'S MINE...
KANDORIAN-- I PROMISE I WILL NOT FORGET YOUR INTERFERENCE...
SSSZZZZZZZZ
LET ME GO!
DAMN YOU! SUPERMAN IS MINE!
...WHILE THE KANDORIAN EMERGENCY SQUAD REMOVES THIS TRANSDIMENSIONAL MISTAKE!
PARALYTIC RAYS AT MAXIMUM!
CERIZAH! KOFF WE KNEW KANDOR MUST HAVE ESCAPED DESTRUCTION, BUT...
BUT WHAT ARE WE DOING HERE?
THAT'S A FAIR QUESTION...

...SECONDS BEFORE THE KRYPTONITE WARHEAD STRUCK YOUR FORTRESS, KANDORIAN REALITY-FLUX SENSORS ALERTED US OF THE IMPENDING DISASTER...
...OUR SCIENTISTS WERE ABLE TO CUT THE TENUOUS CORDS THAT BOUND US TO YOUR PLANE OF REALITY JUST IN TIME.

KANDOR ESCAPED DESTRUCTION, BUT WAS CAST ADRIFT...
...IN THE PHANTOM ZONE!

REMARKABLY, WE FOUND THE CYBORG THERE AS WELL! THE ZONE WOULD SEEM TO BE A SORT OF PROTOCOSMIC CATCH-ALL FOR DIMENSIONAL RIFT DEBRIS.
IRONICALLY, WE'VE BEEN ABLE TO TRACK CYBORG WITHIN THE ZONE WITH THE VERY TECHNOLOGY HE BROUGHT TO KANDOR...
...THE SAME TECHNOLOGY THAT NOW PARALYZES HIM!

BUT WE MUST HURRY BACK-- A TEMPORARY FLUX-STATE SURROUNDING THE RE-CREATION OF YOUR FORTRESS ALLOWED US THIS RARE DEPARTURE FROM KANDOR...
...BUT THAT IS DISAPPEARING AS REMATERIALIZATION APPROACHES COMPLETION.

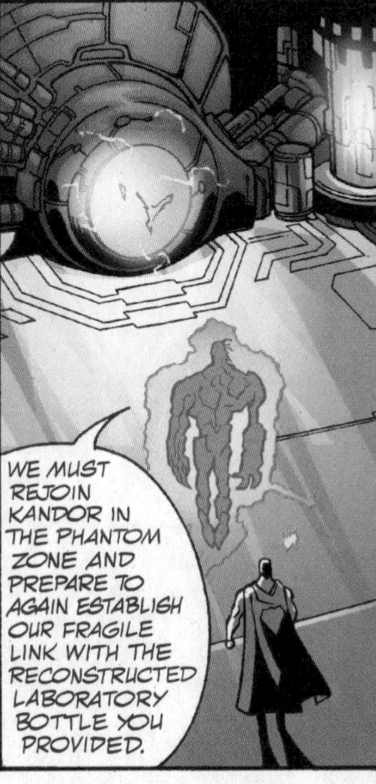
WE MUST REJOIN KANDOR IN THE PHANTOM ZONE AND PREPARE TO AGAIN ESTABLISH OUR FRAGILE LINK WITH THE RECONSTRUCTED LABORATORY BOTTLE YOU PROVIDED.

IF ALL GOES WELL, KANDOR WILL SOON AGAIN RESIDE SAFELY WITHIN YOUR WALLS...
...UNTIL THAT DAY WHEN OUR CITY IS FREED FROM ITS TRANSDIMENSIONAL PRISON!
TILL WE MEET AGAIN, MY FRIEND... KOFF

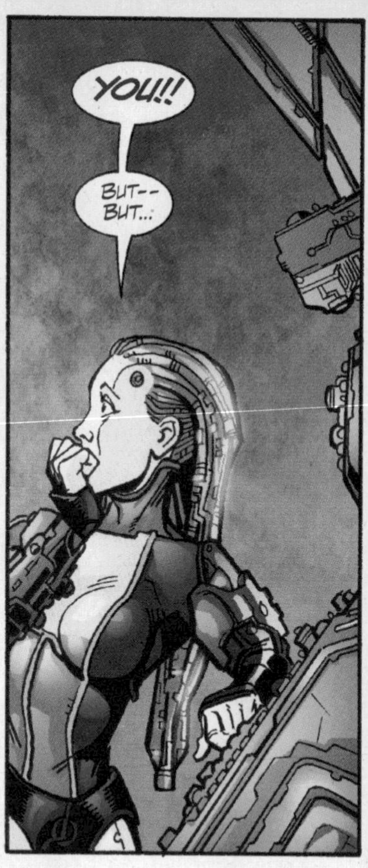

BUT YOU DIDN'T EXPECT TO SEE ME SO SOON?

SKRUUNCH

METHINKS THE CYBORG AND YOU HAVE *PLOTTED* AGAINST MY HOUSE.

KONK

CURSE HIM! WE WERE SO *CLOSE*!

WHERE THE *HELL* IS THE WAY OUT...

NO...

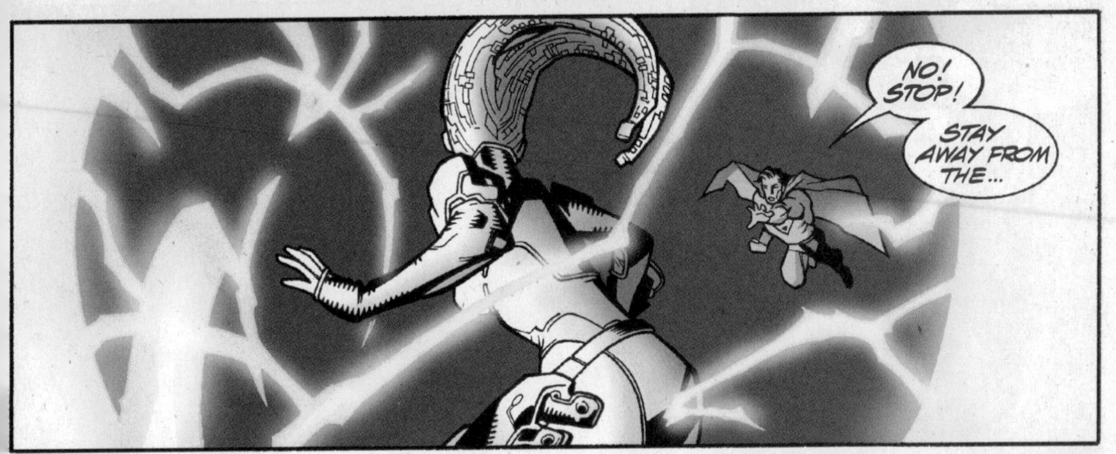
NO! STOP!
STAY AWAY FROM THE...

WHAT'S H-HAPPENING?!
IT'S P-PULLING M-ME-- IN...
...H-HELP ME...

HELP MEEEEE...
HOLD ON!
HOLD...

SHE'S GONE! GOT TO GO IN-- GET HER OUT...
NO, BIG BLUE; IT'S TOO LATE!
YOU CAN'T JUST FLY IN AND NAVIGATE THE PHANTOM ZONE; IT'S NOT LIKE OUR REALITY!

JUST CLOSE THE PORTAL BEFORE ITS TRANSITION FIELD DISRUPTS ANYTHING ELSE!
IF THE GIRL CAN BE RESCUED, IT WILL HAPPEN AT ANOTHER TIME.

ANOTHER TIME, THEN -- BUT I WILL BRING HER BACK.
WHAT'S ≷KOFF≶ OUR STATUS, KELEX?
THE ALIEN OVERRIDE HAS DISSIPATED--WE ARE AGAIN MASTERS OF OUR DOMAIN.
CONSTRUCTION IS 98.783% COMPLETE WITH NO FURTHER COMPLICATIONS ANTICIPATED. BIG...
GOOD. START PHASE 2--BEGIN DOWNLOADING KRYPTONIAN TECHNICAL FILES TO THE STEELWORKS... ≷KOFF≶
...I'VE GOT TO STEP OUTSIDE.

SO MANY OF THEM--THEY DON'T STOP...
IN THE BEGINNING, HE IS THE EARTH-GIANT. IN MORE CIVILIZED TIMES HE BECOMES THE STEEL-DRIVING FOLK HERO JOHN HENRY--THE HERO WHO TAKES ON THE DEHUMANIZING EXCESSES OF AN INDUSTRIAL REVOLUTION THAT THREATENS TO SMOTHER THE WORKING MAN.

IT'S JUST SO VACANT LIVING IN METROPOLIS.
YOU SHOULD NOT HAVE KEPT ME WAITING THIS LONG.
THROOM
THOUGHT YOU'D LEARN TO APPRECIATE ME MORE.
WOW. YOUR UNCLE IS REALLY-- YOU KNOW...
YEAH. HE'S GOOD AT WHAT HE DOES.
KRAK
NICE HEAVE-- OUCH.
THAT'S GONNA LEAVE A MARK.

HOPE THE KIDS GOT OUT OF HERE.
YOU GET ENOUGH ANTS TOGETHER AND THEY'LL BRING DOWN EVEN AN ELEPHANT...
IN SPIRIT, JOHN HENRY WAS AN EARTH-GIANT. BUT IN BODY HE WAS A MAN, AND HIS SUPERHUMAN EFFORTS BROUGHT HIM AN EARLY GRAVE...

...AND THIS ELEPHANT IS WEARING...

SHOOOOM

YOU KNOW, IF YOU GUYS ARE GOING TO STICK WITH THIS INSECT THEME, YOU'RE GOING TO HEAR A LOT OF INFESTATION JOKES...
EEEP.

AND EXTERMINATOR JOKES.
AND THEN IT JUST GETS UGLY.
OKAY, PUNKS-- THE ODDS HAVE EVENED A BIT.
I'VE GOT MY SECOND WIND-- SO COME AND GET IT!
HMMM-- MAYBE THEY FEEL THE TIDE-- <KOFF> HAS TURNED.
AND NONE TOO SOON--MY SECOND WIND DIDN'T LAST VERY LONG.
GOOD LORD, SUPERMAN-- YOU DO NOT LOOK GOOD.
THE FORTRESS?
SAFE, SECURE, OPERATING, AND DOWNLOADING TO YOUR COMPUTERS... <KOFF>
WHICH MEANS I SHOULD BE ABLE TO SECURE THE 'WORKS AGAIN, THANK GOD...
UNC! BORIS AND I NEED SOMETHING TO EAT...

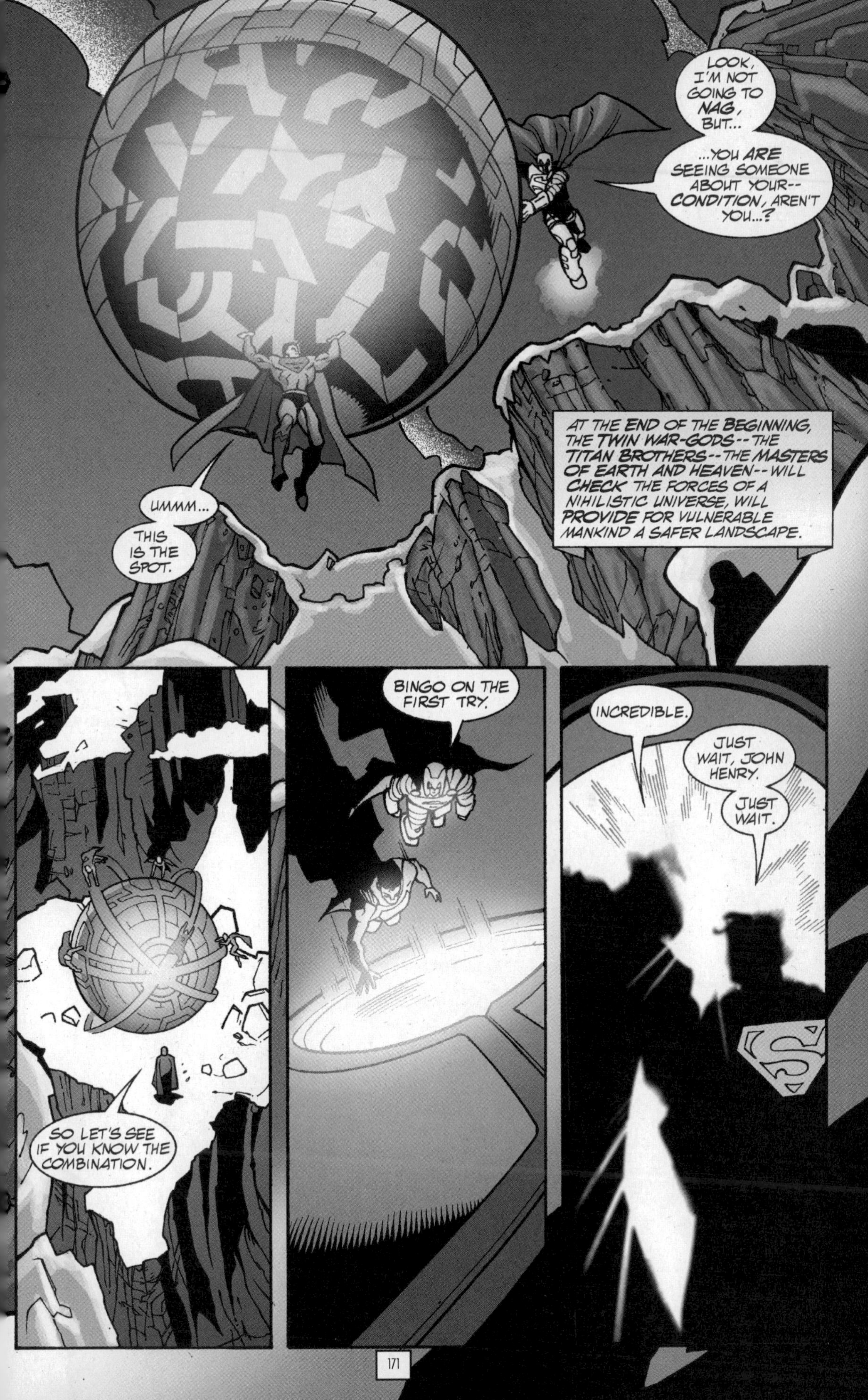
LOOK, I'M NOT GOING TO NAG, BUT...
...YOU ARE SEEING SOMEONE ABOUT YOUR-- CONDITION, AREN'T YOU...?
AT THE END OF THE BEGINNING, THE TWIN WAR-GODS--THE TITAN BROTHERS--THE MASTERS OF EARTH AND HEAVEN--WILL CHECK THE FORCES OF A NIHILISTIC UNIVERSE, WILL PROVIDE FOR VULNERABLE MANKIND A SAFER LANDSCAPE.
UMMM...
THIS IS THE SPOT.
SO LET'S SEE IF YOU KNOW THE COMBINATION.
BINGO ON THE FIRST TRY.
INCREDIBLE.
JUST WAIT, JOHN HENRY.
JUST WAIT.

THANK YOU, JOHN
THANK YOU FOR BRINGING ME BACK TO MY HERITAGE.
THANK YOU FOR GIVING THE WORLD ANOTHER LAYER OF PROTECTION.
LOOKS LIKE A PRETTY SOLID JOB OF CONSTRUCTION.

HEY! I JUST THOUGHT OF SOMETHING...
OH?
IF EVERYTHING REMATERIALIZED, THERE'S SOMETHING I NEED TO GIVE YOU...
WELL, I'LL BE. IT LOOKS LIKE IT IS HERE...
...IT'S NOT EXACTLY A GIFT...
...I MEAN-- *KOFF* YOU'VE CERTAINLY EARNED IT MANY TIMES OVER...
YOUR CAPE.
OUR CAPE.
WE'RE PARTNERS NOW.
I MEAN, I'D BE HONORED IF...
SAY NO MORE-- PARTNER.
THANKS.
"OUR WORK--OUR LIVES-- ARE NOW AS LINKED AS THE COMPUTERS BETWEEN THE FORTRESS AND THE STEELWORKS.
"WE EACH MAKE THE OTHER STRONGER."
NOW-- I NEED TO TALK WITH YOU ABOUT THE INFLUENCE YOUR NIECE IS HAVING ON MY ROBOT...
TOGETHER, THEY HOLD BACK CHAOS A LITTLE BIT LONGER.

METROPOLIS. NOW INARGUABLY THE CITY OF TOMORROW --
...AND THE RAIL WHALE TRAIN! OH! PUT MY EYES OUT WITH A HAIRBRUSH IF THE SUBWAYS IN BROOKLYN SHOULD BE THAT CLEAN!
THOUGH FOR THREE STREET LEVELS AND ALL THE NEW-DO, I STILL CAN'T FIND A DECENT CANNOLI.
-- DESPITE THE RESIDENTS OF THE PRESENT.
FOR THIS, YOU WOULD MOVE? POOPSIE, AUNT BUNNY IS A MORON.
YIP!

YOU SHOULD FALL ON YOUR KNEES TO THANK GOD YOU OWN A SLICE OF THE GREATEST CITY ON EARTH --
NO TIME. I'M TOO BUSY ASKING HIM TO ARRANGE A DATE WITH LEX LUTHOR.
LUTHOR? HA! HON, CALL THE DOCTOR -- HE PULLED TOO TIGHT ON THAT ON THE LAST LIFT.
YIP!

WHY NOT? WE RUB THE SAME ELBOWS! I MET HIM ONCE, AT A BENEFIT THING. A REAL PRESENCE, SO...
...SINGLE.
BUNNY! THE MAN IS IN MOURNING! HE LOST HIS CHILD TO SAVE THIS CITY! HE'S VULNERABLE AND EMPTY AND --

AND WHEN YOU WANT TO MARRY UP AT 40, IT'S A DOG-EAT-DOG WORLD, GLADYS. YOU NEVER LEARNED THAT --
THAT'S WHY MEL RAN OFF WITH THE MONEY GIRL FROM OTB.
YIP YIP YIP YIP YIP
GRRRRRR
CHOMP
ZSA ZSA?
POOPSIE.
OH, DEAR... WOULD YOU LOOK AT THAT?

A CLOWN Comes To METRO
JOE KELLY Writes
KANO Pencils
MARLO ALQUIZA Inks
YOU GOT YOUR POODLE IN MY HYENA -- I GOT MY HYENA ALL OVER YOUR POODLE --
IT'S TWO GREAT DANES THAT DANE GREAT TOGETHER! JOKER'S POODLE-CARCASS CUP!
NOW WHO WANTS TO GET NAKED AND PLAY GLOBAL THERMONUCLEAR SCRABBLE?
"I could really use a laugh these days."
-- Clark Kent, Daily Planet. Mar. 2000
HEEHEEHEEHEEHEE
RICHARD STARKINGS & COMICRAFT Letters
MAUREEN McTIGUE Associate Editor
EDDIE BERGANZA Editor

POLIS
GLENN WHITMORE & WILDSTORM FX Colors
SUPERMAN Created by: JOE SHUSTER and JERRY SIEGEL
G-GOD -- P-PLEASE --
YOU TWO LOOK LIKE MODELS, YOU KNOW THAT?
MODEL T'S, TO BE EXACT... AFTER THE HEAD-ON COLLISION -- EXACTLY THE LOOK I'M LOOKING AT! HARLEY!
EASY BOYS... THERE'S PLENTY POOCH FOR EVERYONE.
PEOPLE. PEOPLE! GASP IN TERROR THIS WAY. 'KAY? EYES ON. THE SASSY SIDEKICK IN SPANDEX AND SAY --
PSHWO
--"I WENT TO METROPOLIS AND ALL I GOT FOR IT WAS TO KILL A FEW MILLION PEOPLE!"
OMP
IF YOU RETINAS START TO CRACK, DON'T BE SHY, LICKING EYEBALLS IS MY SPECIALTY.
BLAH BLAH BLAH... BLAH BLAH BLAH...
WAVE TO THE NICE READERS, GIRLS, THEY'RE PAYING THE RENT.

HSSSSSSSS
HSSSSSSS
KLIK
DO YOU HAVE ANY IDEA HOW DISGUSTING IT IS WAKING UP EVERY MORNING TO THE SMELL OF BURNING HAIR?
I --
NO... I NEVER THOUGHT --
OR COURSE YOU DIDN'T. GOD FORBID YOU SHOULD TAKE THE LITTLE EARTH GIRL YOU MARRIED INTO CONSIDERATION.
LOIS --
NO, GET OUT OF HERE, CLARK. I GOTTA GO...
AND SPRAY SOMETHING, WOULD YOU? PLACE STINKS.

"THEY CERTAINLY WERE WELL PREPARED IN THE FUTURE, WEREN'T THEY?
"WHAT DOES *THIS BUTTON* DO?"
FAR AS WE CAN TELL, SIR, THAT ONE ACCESSES *TELECOM SATELLITES.*
WHICH SATELLITES?
ALL OF THEM, SIR, *WORLD-WIDE.*
SPLENDID. AND THIS?
WAIT!
UH-- HEH-- THAT SWITCH APPARENTLY CAUSES THE CHAIRS AROUND THE CONFERENCE TABLE TO FLIP *BACKWARDS...*
...DUMPING ITS OCCUPANTS THROUGH A FLOOR PANEL DOWN THROUGH A *CHUTE* INTO A *VAT OF ACID*, SIR.
THIS IS A *JOKE?*
NO, SIR. WE LOST TWO MEN TODAY BEFORE WE RESTUDIED THE *SCHEMATICS*.

HMM. JUST WHEN I THOUGHT THE LUTHORS COULDN'T STOOP ANY *LOWER*. MY *SUCCESSOR* INSTALLS *DEATH TRAPS* INTO THE BOARD ROOM.
I *LOVE* THE FUTURE.

BLAH BLAH BLAH...
I'M *SO SMART...* I DRESS WELL IN ITALIAN *CRAVATS* AND EAT FOOD WITH *FRENCH NAMES.*
WHO IS THAT?

MY HEAD IS SO BIG IT OUTGREW MY *HAIR.*
I'M *LEX LUTHOR...* HEAR ME BORE.

MONTREAL, CANADA.
NEVER SEEN HIM LIKE THAT. YOU THINK HE'S ALL RIGHT?
...SHOULD START ANY SECOND...
...NEW TRADE AGREEMENTS...
...FEED IS GOOD? GREAT. HOPE THE CONFERENCE IS WORTH IT.
GOT A BUD, WORKS COPY DOWN AT THE DAILY PLANET. SAYS THERE'S "TROUBLE IN PARADISE."
HMMMM. HOPE I NEVER GET THAT SORT OF TROUBLE... LOOKS WORSE THAN --
HNNNNZZHH
PATHETIC.
SNORT HUH -- WHAZZA -- BUH -- I'M SORRY, LOIS, WHAT CAN I -- ?
...
HEH... NO ONE BOUGHT ALASKA WHILE I WAS ASLEEP. RIGHT? HEH. I -- UH -- AH--
ZEE-ZEE-ZEE-ZEE-ZEE-ZEE-ZEE-ZEE-ZEE-ZEE-Z
AH CHOO!
COUGH
BLEARGH
NOTHING TO SEE HERE, FOLKS... JUST A MILD-MANNERED REPORTER WITH A TOUCH OF THE FLU...
AND A FISTFUL OF TROUBLE... AT HOME...?
HOME. JIMMY. OH, BOY.
ZEE-ZEE-ZEE-ZEE-ZEE-ZEE-ZEE-ZEE-ZEE-ZEE-ZEE-

I THOUGHT Y2K FIXED THE SIGNAL WATCH. IF SUPERMAN'S NOT HERE BY NOW, SOMETHING'S UP, LOIS.
YOU COULD SAY THAT AGAIN.
ZEE-ZEE-ZEE-ZEE-ZEE
PSHWOOP
SAY FROMAGE!
BLAH BLAH BLAH... I'M LEX LUTHOR! BALD IS BEAUTIFUL... BLAH BLAH BLAH...
"AMUSING, JOKER. SINCERELY. CEASE IMMEDIATELY AND I'LL SIMPLY CONSIDER IT AN ILL-CONCEIVED PERVERSION OF A FRIAR'S CLUB ROAST."
QUIT BEFORE WE'VE DELIVERED THE PUNCH LINE? FOR SHAME!
KI-KLAKK
I DUNNO, BALDY. PERHAPS IT WAS THE MUSE OF MADNESS, BETTY, WHO DOTH BE LOWERED ON A SILKEN BUNGEE CORD AND WHISPER GUMDROPS OF POISON INTO MINE CAMEL EARS --
SIGH AMATEURS. NO SPIRIT OF NUANCE.
-- MAYBE I HAD ONE TOO MANY OF HARLEY'S CAFFEINE, SUGAR M.S.G. PARFAITS --
TEE HEE. ME AM STEALTHY.
PS
CHOMP
I'M LUTHOR... I CAN BUY YOUR GRANDMOTHER FOR BREAKFAST AND SELL BOTH HER HIPS BY LUNCHTIME... I USE SPARKLY TOOTHPASTE. I HAVE A VEAL PILLOW...
OR MAYBE YOU SHOULD HAVE KEPT YOUR DAMN HANDS OUT OF GOTHAM. QUID PRO QUO, BIPPY. YOU CASA MI CASA.
IT'S A FREE WORLD, MANIAC. GUARDS, MY LIFE HAS BEEN THREATENED. DEADLY FORCE AUTHORIZED.

I PUT A LOT OF BLUT, SCHVITZ UND EYEJUICE INTO THIS LITTLE SOIREE! SEE?
I MURDERED A DINNER THEATRE WILLY LOMAN FOR HIS BALD WIG AND EVERYTHING!
WHY?
FUNNY GIRL IS MINE!
OOOH! ME FIRST?! I'M A REPRESSED CHAUFFEUR WITH NO HOPE OF UPWARD PROMOTION AND I HATE MYSELF!
CATFIGHT!
I'VE GOT A BALL OF YARN! WHO'S GOT MILK?!
STOP.
I DON'T REQUIRE YOUR ASSISTANCE HERE, ALIEN.
BEGONE.
DO I KNOW YOU?
OH, WAIT! UNDERWEAR-ON-THE-OUTSIDE LAD! SORRY, THIS IS A PRIVATE MOCKERY. BUH-BYE.

I'M NOT ASK ✳KAFF✳
I'M NOT ASKING.
PARDON MY FRENCH, BLUE BOY, BUT YOU LOOK LIKE A BUFFET TABLE AFTER A SENIOR CITIZENS'S EARLY BIRD SPECIAL!
WHAT HAPPENED? JUST FILED YOUR TAX RETURN?
I SAID LEAVE, ALIEN.
NOT A CHANCE --
ESPECIALLY NOT AFTER A BLASÉ COMMAND LIKE THAT, LEXXIE! LET'S SEE A LITTLE STYLE! A LITTLE VA-VOOM!
LIKE SO.
FURFEEET
BOYS, WOULD YOU PLEASE SERVE OUR MAN SUPES WITH A CEASE-AND-DESIST BREATHING ORDER?
HEEHEEHAHAHEEE
WHOULFF!
SLASHH
ARRRGH!
GOOD PUPPY, GO BITEY.
YOU HURT HIM? WITH HYENAS?
MAKES YOU RECONSIDER BELIEVING IN MIRACLES, DON'T IT?

STAGE I
MERCY VS HARLEY
ROUND I
TRAMP.
SILICON BARBIE.
HEY, LOOK. FREAKS.
CHICK FREAKS.
WOW. YEAH.
DON'T YOU JUST HATE IT WHEN YOU SHOW UP TO THE MASSACRE AND REALIZE THAT YOUR VICTIM IS WEARING THE SAME OUTFIT?
YOU'RE GOING TO DIE.
"REPRESSED DOMINATRIX" REALLY ISN'T MY STYLE, THOUGH. SOME GIRLS CAN GET AWAY WITH IT--
-- YOU. STARFIRE, BIG BARDA--
HRRGH!
poink poink
LUCKILY, I WENT TO FINISHING SCHOOL. I CAN MAKE PETIT FOURS.
KIEYAHH!
WHAT DO YOU HAVE TO FALL BACK ON, MERCY... BESIDES YOUR BACK, THAT IS?
SLASH
OOPSIE!
THAT'S WHAT I THOUGHT.

LEXXIE, SWEETCHEEKS, I HAVEN'T TRIPPED THE LIGHT FANDANGO WITH SUPERMAN IN A DOG'S AGE --

--BUT I REMEMBER HIM BEING MORE... ROBUST. MORE HESTON THAN HERMAN?

UNQUESTIONABLY, COMMENDABLE WORK. PSIONICALLY CONTROLLED CYBERNETIC CONSTRUCTS?

YOU HAVE *ACID* ON YOUR *CHIN.*
HRRARGH!
THAT'S ENOUGH!
FSCHOWW
YIPE YIPE YIPE YIPE YIPE YIPE
BETTER THAN A *KOFF* ROLLED-UP *NEWSPAPER.*
YOU SOUND A LITTLE *TICKED --*
KAFF KOFF
--OFF?
SWIFF

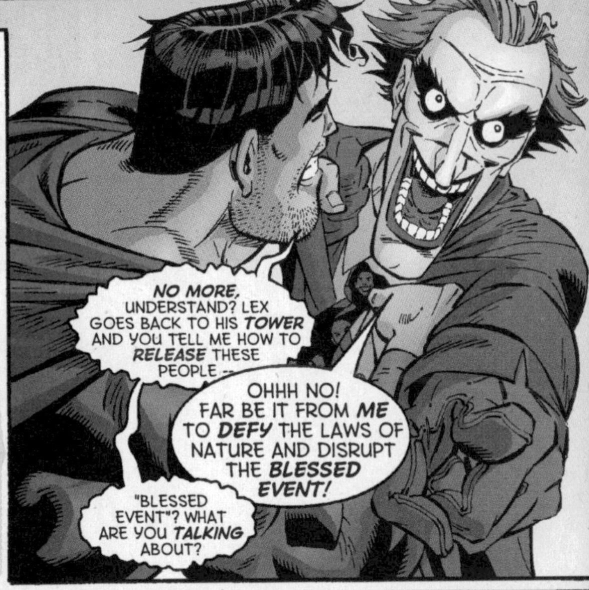

"ONCE UPON A TIMEBOMB, A CERTAIN HAIR-CHALLENGED TYRANT TRIED TO REDECORATE MY GOTHAM CITY IN HIS IMAGE --

"-- BUT IT TURNS OUT THAT LEX'S SELF-IMAGE IS IN THE DUMPER SINCE NEW YEAR'S. THOSE BEADY LITTLE EYES HAD LOST THEIR SHINE.

"I TELL YOU, SUPES... I'M NOT PRONE TO HYSTERICS, BUT SEEING LI'L LEX SO LOW JUST TORE ME TO TWITCHING BLOODY PIECES!
"SEEING AS WE'RE SUCH CHUMS, I THOUGHT I'D BRING HIM A LITTLE PICK ME UP! SOMETHING TO HELP HIM THROUGH THE ROUGH SPOTS.

"WITNESS... REBIRTH!"
LENA
CHRMMBLE
WHY DID YOU LET ME DIE, DADDY? WHY DID I DIE, DADDY?! I'M DEAD BUT I LOVE YOU, DADDY!

YOU MONSTER.
OH NO... I'M JUST A MAN LIKE ANY OTHER, TRYING TO BRING AN INFANTICIST AND THE ROBOTIC EMBODIMENT OF HIS DECEASED CHILD TOGETHER.
P.S. WE SHOULD MOVE NOW.

PA
DOOOM
HNNNGH!
AH, THE LITTLE SCAMP! ISN'T SHE PRECIOUS, LEX? ZINC LOZENGE, SUPERMAN?
KAFF KOFF GOD, MAN... THE MADNESS. WHY?
WHY? CALL ME CRAZY, BUT I THINK IT'S A PIP THE WAY KIDS ALWAYS SEEM TO DIE OR GET SHOT IN THE SPINE!
YOU -- KAFF COUGH KOFF
HEY, WHY DON'T I LEAVE YOU TO HACK UP A LUNG AND TALK DIAPER CHANGES WITH LEX?
PLAYMATES HAVE ARRIVED.
HUKK LEX... KOFF LEX... WHAT HE'S DOING TO YOU -- I WOULDN'T WISH IT ON ANYONE.
DO NOT PITY ME, SUPERMAN, PITY THE CLOWN.
BY THE WAY, HE'S AT IT AGAIN.
I'LL SAY IT WITH PUPPETS, SINCE I KNOW THEY LOWERED THE CURVE ON THE M.P.D. ENTRANCE EXAM --
"DIPLOMATIC IMMUNITY IS A GAS!" RIGHT, SHEIK? LET'S SHOW THEM HOW WE PARTY BACK IN QURAC!

STAGE 2

MERCY vs HARLEY ROUND 2

TEAR OUT YOUR SPLEEN AND SHOVE IT IN YOUR -- MOUTH!

HAPPY HUMP DAY!
FWASSSH

FIRE!
BLAM BLAM
BLAM BLAM
YEARRGH!

I SAID SHUT UP!
... GENTLEMEN? *KFF* *KOFF* MAYBE YOU COULD LET ME HANDLE THIS?

BACK IN QURAQ! I HIT THE SACK! S'BEEN SO LONG I'M GLAD TO BE BACK!
STOP IT.

I SOLD MY SOUL TO ROCK AND ROLL. AC-DC FOREVER.
CRUNNCH
I SAID SHUT UP!

DEAR GOD IN HEAVEN! LOOK WHAT YOU DID TO MY HAND!
I -- OH --

WHY ME DIE, DA DA?! WHY ME DIE?!
LENA
SMASHH

THE INHUMANITY! YOU MONSTER! AND AFTER WHAT THAT NASTY COMMISSIONER DID TO MY LEG IN GOTHAM!
YOU'LL LIVE. STAY PUT, MAYBE I'LL GET YOU TO A DOCTOR.
THREATENING TO WITHHOLD MEDICAL CARE? HA!
HOW VERY DARK KNIGHT OF YOU!
ONLY THERE'S A DIFFERENCE! BATMAN GETS THE JOKE --!

"-- HE KNOWS WE'RE ALL A LITTLE SICK! BUT WHILE HE WRAPS HIS ISSUES UP IN A UTILITY BELT AND VOILA -- VENGEANCE --
LENA
FWHAMMM
"-- YOU'RE LETTING YOUR SICKNESS EAT YOU ALIVE."
"I DON'T FEEL VERY GOOD.
"JUST BEING CLOSE TO... THE JOKER... ILL...
"LOIS. LOIS'S EYES... SO ANGRY... SO... SICK...
"DID SOMETHING JUST HIT ME?"
CHOOM
JUST... A FEW MORE MINUTES, MA... A LITTLE REST.
HELP?

SHAZZAKKATTA
DADDIEEEEEZT
THOOM
BLAH BLAH... I'M LEX... HUH?
BALD?
WHAT HAPPENED --?
STUPID DANG NAB QURAQI PARTS --
AUTOMATIC CAMEL WATERER -- NO PROBLEMO! ASK FOR A GIANT DEATH-DOLLY, AND THE CRAFTSMANSHIP JUST DETERIORATES!
SUPERMAN! IT WORKED!
NO CLUE WHAT YOU PULLED FROM YOUR BAG OF TRICKS, BUT --
I -- I DIDN'T DO ANYTHING... COULDN'T... WHAT HAPPENED?
LEX LUTHOR SAVES METROPOLIS AGAIN.

LEXCORP
THE LEXCORP OF THE FUTURE IS MORE THAN A SYMBOL OF POWER --
--IT IS POWER.
WITH THE FLIP OF A SWITCH, A BROADBAND SIGNAL TRANSMITTED ON ALL FREQUENCIES NOT SANCTIONED BY LEXCORP CARRIES CODES THAT ESSENTIALLY REBOOT ELECTRICAL EQUIPMENT.
MODALITIES "NOT SANCTIONED" INCLUDE GIANT ROBOTS. QURAQI PARTS. AND MOST HUMAN BRAINS.
YOUR PERSECUTION OF METROPOLIS'S POOR CITIZENS IS OVER, JOKER.
WELL, AREN'T WE A MEGALOMANIACAL MacGYVER? BRAVO, LEXXIE.
MAYBE YOU CAN MAKE A BRINX TRUCK OUT OF A BANANA PEEL AND SOME DUCT TAPE AND RUN YOURSELF OVER WITH IT.
I WILL NOT BE HELD HOSTAGE IN MY OWN CITY, EVER. YOU WANTED TO SEE METROPOLIS? MY METROPOLIS?
YOU'VE SEEN IT. METROPOLIS IS LUTHOR.
NOW GET OUT BEFORE MY CITY SPITS YOU OUT.
SNAKT
I HAVE TO HAND IT TO YOU, LEXXIE...
...A STUNT LIKE THAT AT THE ELEVENTH HOUR --
--YOU'RE ALMOST AS CRAZY AS I AM! WE OUGHTA SWAP MEDS SOMETIME.
SNAP
FOR NOW, THOUGH, MY ENTOURAGE AND I HAVE HAD ENOUGH OF LOVELY METROPOLIS.
WE REALLY PREFER DOMINATING CITIES WITH MORE SAND --
-- BUT I DO WANT TO CORRECT YOU ON ONE THING...

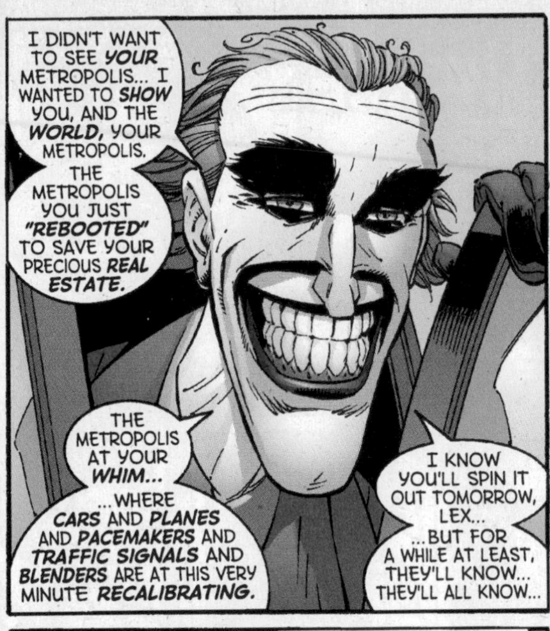
I DIDN'T WANT TO SEE YOUR METROPOLIS... I WANTED TO SHOW YOU, AND THE WORLD, YOUR METROPOLIS.
THE METROPOLIS YOU JUST "REBOOTED" TO SAVE YOUR PRECIOUS REAL ESTATE.
THE METROPOLIS AT YOUR WHIM...
...WHERE CARS AND PLANES AND PACEMAKERS AND TRAFFIC SIGNALS AND BLENDERS ARE AT THIS VERY MINUTE RECALIBRATING.
I KNOW YOU'LL SPIN IT OUT TOMORROW, LEX...
...BUT FOR A WHILE AT LEAST, THEY'LL KNOW... THEY'LL ALL KNOW...

THAT A LUNATIC IS RUNNING THEIR ASYLUM.
SCREEECH
CRASH
POOM

WAIT, YOU CAN'T JUST --
SORRY, SWEETHEART, BUT THIS BIRD'S GOTTA FLY! IPLOMATIC DIMMUNITY, YOU KNOW!

VRMMMM
NO. TWO MINUTES, I'LL FLY YOU TO CANADA WHERE QURAQ DOESN'T HAVE ANY IMMUNITY, AND --
BLUE, SERIOUSLY. YOU'RE FRIGHTENING THE LADIES BESIDES...

...I'M ALL FOR IMPROVISATION, AND I'LL BE THE FIRST TO ADMIT THAT THE D.I. GAG WILL ONLY PLAY FOR SO LONG --♡
-- BUT I WASN'T KIDDING ABOUT THE AIRPLANES.
FIFTY SECONDS LEFT. IF YOU'RE NOT GOING TO LIE DOWN FOR ANOTHER NAPPY.
DIPOLMATIC IMMUNITY. BEGINNING IN BIRDS OF PREY #16 -- ED.

IS HE SERIOUS? CAN... CAN HE DO THAT?
HA HA HA HA HA HA
SCREEECH
HE JUST DID.

STAGE 3
-- PLAY PING PONG WITH YOUR EYES --
MERCY vs HARLEY
ROUND 3
COTTON CANDY? CRUNCHY!

SWOOSH
HFF YOU... H-HAD ENOUGH PFF CLOWN?
I CAN DO THIS KAFF ALL NIGHT KOFF BEANPOLE --
H-HEY... WHAT'S THAT BEHIND YOU?
OH, PLEASE --
BEEP BEEP
OH, NO.
WHAM
I SMELL FUN DIP!
HARL, BE A FALL DOLL AND DO SOMETHING ABOUT M.P.D., WOULD YOU?
MAKE MY EXCUSES, PEN MY GOODBYES, AND DO MY JAIL TIME UNTIL THINGS COOL OFF?
P-PUDDIN...?
YOU'RE A PRINCESS. I'M OFF WITH ALIA AND FRIEND HERE FOR A THOUSAND AND ONE ARABIAN NIGHTS OF FUN!
MEN, D'OH.
YEAH... MEN.
BUBBLE BUTT.
BIMBO.

DAILY PLA
FOR PITY'S SAKE, KENT! I ADMIRE DEDICATION, BUT GET THEE TO A DOCTOR!
I WILL, PERRY *SNF* BUT AFTER BOTCHING THE CANADA THING *COUGH* I HAVE TO FILE THIS ONE...
IMAGINE THE LUCK THAT I WAS ON THE PLANE SUPERMAN CAUGHT! *KOFF* OPPORTUNITY KNOCKING --
ACHOO!
YOU'VE GOT A STRANGE DEFINITION OF "LUCK," KENT...
CLARK... I DON'T WANT TO CROSS A LINE HERE, BUT... DO YOU HAVE A PLACE TO STAY TONIGHT? A NON-COUCH PLACE?
HEH, THANKS, PERRY, BUT I'M OKAY. DIFFICULT AS THINGS ARE *KAFF* THEY HAVEN'T GONE DOWN THAT ROAD YET --
PIZZA FOR KENT!
HEY! WATCH IT! I DIDN'T ORDER ANY PIZZA --
NOPE, YOU DIDN'T --
-- BUT SOME HOTTY IN THE LOBBY GAVE ME TWENTY BUCKS TO HAND THIS TO YOU.
WHAT?!
DON'T THINK IT'S GOOD, BUT WHAT DO I KNOW ABOUT LOVE? LATER.
IT'S A NOTE... LOIS'S HANDWRITING --
"DEAR CLARK... CAN'T FACE YOU... DON'T LOOK FOR ME..."
"THE LIVING ROOM ISN'T FAR ENOUGH AWAY..."
"I'M LEAVING..." FOREVER?

DEAR MA AND PA, THIS LETTER IS PROBABLY THE HARDEST THING I'VE EVER HAD TO DO.
I'VE THOUGHT ABOUT FLYING BACK TO SMALLVILLE TO TELL YOU WHAT HAS HAPPENED...
...BUT, I STILL NEED SOME TIME TO SORT THIS OUT.
I WISH IT WERE SOME SORT OF APRIL FOOL'S JOKE OR THAT I'LL WAKE UP AND IT'S ALL BEEN A HORRIBLE NIGHTMARE.
LOIS IS LEAVING ME...

I WENT TO OUR CLOSEST FRIENDS TO SEE IF SOMEHOW, I DON'T KNOW, I DID SOMETHING WRONG AS A HUSBAND.

PERRY. JIMMY. EVEN HER SISTER LUCY AND RON. THEY ALL TALKED LIKE...

...LIKE IT ALL CAME OUT OF THE BLUE.

FOR ONCE, CLARK, I DON'T KNOW WHAT TO SAY.

I THOUGHT IT WAS ALL ABOUT YOU BEING MADE FOREIGN CORRESPONDENT --

-- BUT YOU'VE **ALWAYS** TRAVELED OR BEEN ON ASSIGNMENT AND LOIS COULD HANDLE IT...

THIS SUCKS!

YOU GUYS EVEN HAD **ME** THINKING THAT BEING MARRIED COULD BE, Y'KNOW, KINDA COOL.

HAVE YOU TALKED TO **SUPERMAN?** HE AND LOIS SEEM PRETTY CLOSE --

-- I MEAN, LIKE FRIENDS...

TELL YOU THE TRUTH, CLARK, WE'VE BEEN SO WRAPPED UP IN OUR **OWN** PROBLEMS --

THE BABY. GETTING -- UM -- MARRIED. WE DIDN'T SEE THIS COMING AT ALL.

BUT, LOIS DOESN'T REALLY CONFIDE IN US, CLARK. THAT'S JUST HOW SHE IS.

SUPERMA
ENE
LO

JEPH LOEB
Writer

ED McGUINNESS
Pencils

CAM S
Ink

RICHARD STARKINGS
Letters

MAUREEN McTIGUE
Associate Editor

EDDIE BERGAN
Editor

I'VE EVEN FOUND MYSELF HOPING THIS WAS SOME SORT OF WILD SCHEME TO GET BACK AT SUPERMAN.
MAYBE IT WAS LUTHOR. OR BRAINIAC 13. OR MXYZPTLK. BUT, HOW, AND WHY AND GETTING LOIS TO BE PART OF IT...
NO, I HAD TO ACCEPT THIS FOR WHAT IT WAS.
I ALWAYS THOUGHT IT WAS ONLY KRYPTONITE THAT COULD HURT SUPERMAN.
NOT A BROKEN HEART...
5:06
LANE
TANYA & RICHARD HORIE Colors
Superman created by JERRY SIEGEL JOE and SHUSTER

I COULDN'T SEEM TO CONCENTRATE FROM MOMENT TO MOMENT.
HELLO...?
LOIS...? WHEN DID YOU GET BACK?
I'M JUST PICKING UP SOME OF MY THINGS, CLARK, AND I'LL BE OUT OF HERE.
ALL MY ENERGY WAS SPENT RERUNNING CONVERSATIONS IN MY HEAD THAT MIGHT GIVE ME SOME CLUE.
AND ALL I COULD REMEMBER WAS HER SMILE.
WE HAVE TO TALK.
I KNOW WE'VE GOT SOME THINGS TO WORK OUT.
I MAY SOMETIMES FORGET THE STRAIN I PUT ON OUR MARRIAGE WITH MY HAVING TO BE AT TWELVE PLACES AT ONCE, BUT --
-- YOU HAVE TO BELIEVE ME WHEN I SAY THERE IS NO GREATER PRIORITY THAN US.
WE'RE WAY PAST TALKING, CLARK.

WHERE... WHERE'S YOUR WEDDING RING?
PLEASE TAKE YOUR HAND OFF ME.
ARE YOU HUNGRY? I COULD MAKE US SOME BEEF BOURGUIGNON WITH KETCHUP.
IS THAT SUPPOSED TO BE CLEVER?
WHAT DO YOU THINK, THAT YOU'RE DEALING WITH MY EVIL TWIN?
YOU DIDN'T ANSWER THE QUESTION.
NO, I'M NOT HUNGRY.
AND YES, I KNOW OUR STUPID SECRET PASSWORD IS "BEEF BOURGUIGNON WITH KETCHUP."
AND ALSO HOW IT'S YOUR FAVORITE MEAL.
CLARK.
I'M NOT GOING TO ASK YOU AGAIN.
TAKE YOUR HAND OFF ME.

NOW!

THEN, ALL AT ONCE, WHEN SHE HIT ME...
...I NEVER FELT BETTER IN MY LIFE.

KRASCH
DICKIE, THOSE KENTS ARE AT IT AGAIN.
MARGE, ENOUGH IS ENOUGH. THIS IS THE MOST OUT--
--RAGEOUS...
YOU CAN'T KNOW WHAT I'VE HAD TO PUT UP WITH!
THE NUMBER OF TIMES YOU'VE HUMILIATED ME!
MA AND PA, SHE COULD FLY. THAT WONDERFUL GAL OF MINE COULD FLY AND KICK LIKE A MULE.
AND THAT MEANT ONLY ONE THING --
-- AFTER ALL THIS TIME... THE BITTERNESS... THE WAY SHE'S BEEN ACTING...
... SHE WASN'T OUR LOIS LANE!

BUT... WHO OR WHAT WAS SHE?
IF YOU THINK I'M GOING TO GO EASY ON YOU BECAUSE OF THE FEELINGS I MIGHT'VE ONCE HAD FOR YOU --
-- FORGET IT.
I HAD TO BE CAREFUL. IF LOIS HAD BEEN POSSESSED BY ANOTHER BEING, THEN IT WAS HER REAL BODY I WAS FIGHTING.
CLEARLY, YOU'RE NOT A ROBOT.
I CAN SEE HOW YOU'VE SOMEHOW MANAGED TO MATCH HER SKELETAL STRUCTURE.
BONE FOR BONE.
LOIS TOLD ME ONCE THAT SHE FELL OFF HER BIKE AS A KID WHILE DELIVERING NEWSPAPERS. SHE BROKE HER WRIST. IT NEVER HEALED PROPERLY, LEAVING A HAIRLINE FRACTURE.
IT'S STILL THERE.
YOU'VE GOT HER LOOKS.
HER VOICE.
EVEN HER MEMORIES.
BUT, YOU ARE NOT LOIS.
WHO ARE YOU?
YOU STILL DON'T GET IT --

-- IT'S REALLY ME, SMALLVILLE!

CURIOUS...
GET DOWN!
ZZRAKK
ARE YOU ALL RIGHT, SIR?
APPARENTLY.
MERCY.
BY THE END OF TODAY, I WANT TO KNOW WHO THAT -- THAT "LOIS" IS --
-- AND HOW "SHE" IS RELATED TO MISS LANE'S LATE-NIGHT VISIT TO THIS OFFICE.

I'M GLAD YOU COULD FIND TIME TO STOP BY THE PLANET. I KNOW YOU'VE GOT A LOT OF OTHER PROJECTS TO LOOK AFTER.
PERRY, GIVEN THE HEADACHE WE'RE GOING TO CAUSE LUTHOR, I'LL *MAKE* TIME.
SO, EVERYTHING RUNNING SMOOTHLY? YOUR BALANCE SHEET SEEMS PRETTY HEALTHY.
IT'S LIKE STARTING UP ALL OVER, AGAIN. THERE'S BOUND TO BE GROWING --

I HADN'T BEEN... FEELING ALL THAT WELL LATELY. I DON'T WANT THAT TO CONCERN YOU -- SINCE I'M SURE MOST OF IT WAS THE EMOTIONAL DRAIN OF WHAT HAD BEEN HAPPENING.
WHOOPH
FIGHT ME, SMALLVILLE.
THE THOUGHT OF LIVING IN A WORLD WITHOUT LOIS TO COME HOME TO WAS...
I WANT YOU TO GIVE ME EVERYTHING YOU'VE GOT.
ZZRAKK
FWOOSH
...OVERWHELMING.

BUT... IN THE HEAT OF THE CONFLICT...
EVERYONE WILL KNOW THAT IT WAS ME THAT PUT YOU DOWN.
FWAK
AND RIGHT ABOUT THEN, ALL I COULD FOCUS ON WERE HER INCREDIBLE POWERS.
...SOMETIMES THAT'S WHEN I CAN THINK THE CLEAREST.
STOK
OTHERS HAVE TRIED.
BOIFF
Welcome to METRO
The City of Tom
YOU THINK YOU CAN PLAY "ROPE A DOPE" AND TIRE ME OUT?

I CAN POUND AND POUND ON YOU ALL DAY LONG!
BAM
NNGGGN!

YOU'VE KEPT ME DISTRACTED --
-- MAKING IT LOOK LIKE YOU'VE GOT THE SAME POWERS AS ME.
BUT UP 'TIL NOW I DIDN'T NOTICE IT --
-- THEY'RE NOT THE SAME. YOU REALLY DO HAVE MY POWERS.
YOU IDIOT! WE'RE HEADED RIGHT FOR THE TUN --
BDOOOM

WHAT WAS IT YOU SAID TO ME?
"EVER SINCE I CAME IN CONTACT WITH STRANGE VISITOR, I CAN KEEP OTHER PEOPLE'S POWERS."
ZZRAKK
GET UP.
DON'T YOU WANT IT TO BE YOU WHO DEFEATS ME?
EVERYONE IS GOING TO THINK IT'S LOIS LANE AND NOT YOU --
NO!

PARASITE!
RUDY, NO! SHIFT BACK TO LOIS -- YOU'LL LOSE THE PSYCHOLOGICAL EDGE!
NO! THE WORLD HAS TO KNOW IT'S ME!
THE WEAKNESS I'VE BEEN FEELING.
-KAFF KAFF-
YOU'VE BEEN DRAINING ME FOR HOW LONG?
HOW LONG HAVE YOU PRETENDED TO BE LOIS?

RUDY, I'VE WARNED YOU ABOUT EXERTING YOURSELF.
YAH TOOK IT ALL FROM ME. NOW YAH'LL GET WHAT YAH DESERVE.
I'M SCARED. I WANNA GO HOME.
PLEASE. I JUST WANT TO FIND MY CHILDREN!
SHUT UP! SHUT UP, ALL OF YOU!
RUDY, LET'S GO -- NOW. YOU'RE WEAKENING TOO, CAN'T YOU TELL?
SMASH
CLARK...?
NAW, I GOTTA DO THIS.
YOU ALL MIGHT BE IN MY HEAD, BUT NONE OF YOU KNOWS WHAT IT'S LIKE TO BE ME!
I GOTTA FINISH HIM!
CLARK...?
RUDY!

EVERYTHING!
I STILL LOVE YOU, CLARK. I ALWAYS WILL...
ACKKKK!
BVRAK
PHLOP
LOIS.
WHERE IS LOIS?

I COULD HEAR HIS HEART GROWING FAINTER AND FAINTER.
...W-WAS THE PROFESSOR'S IDEA.
I'VE GOT TO GET YOU TO S.T.A.R. LABS --
DON'T! JUST... JUST LISTEN TO ME, CLARK. NO TIME...
N-NEW YEAR'S. THE POWER FAILURE. GOT FREE...
...WENT TO FIND ANYONE WHO KNEW ABOUT YOU... GET YOUR PSYCHOLOGICAL, YOU KNOW, WEAKNESSES...
...SECRETS...
...STALKED LOIS AND JIMMY... ON THE STREET AND... AND TOUCHED HER... NEVER REALIZING SHE KNEW IT ALL...
STRANGE... VISITOR... CHANGED MY POWER... SO I COULD KEEP WHAT I TOOK LONGER...
...HAD CONTACT WITH SOMEONE... NOT SURE WHO... WHO COULD SHAPE-SHIFT...
...PROFESSOR TOLD ME I COULD MATCH... ANY D.N.A....
VOICE... MEMORIES... A P-ERFECT MA...TCH.
...I BECAME A TRUE PARASITE... TOOK LOIS'S IDENTITY...
...ALL I WANTED WAS TO KILL YOU... MAKE A NAME FOR MYSELF... LIKE DOOMSDAY...
...NOW... WHAT'S KILLING YOU... IS KILLING ME...
RUDY.
IS LOIS STILL ALIVE?
OR DID YOU ABSORB HER COMPLETELY LIKE YOU DID THE PROFESSOR?
...HAD TO... TOUCH HER AGAIN... EVERY TWENTY-FOUR HOURS...
SHE... LOVES YOU...
...LIKE NOBODY EVER LOVED ME...

IT DIDN'T TAKE SUPER HEARING TO TELL --
-- THE PARASITE WAS DEAD.
DON'T KNOW WHY HE TOLD ME ANYTHING. MAYBE THERE WAS JUST A LITTLE TOO MUCH LOIS IN HIM AFTER ALL.
WHERE IS SHE?!
NOTHING ELSE MATTERS TO ME NOW. IF I HAVE TO TEAR APART METROPOLIS BRICK BY BRICK, I WILL FIND MY WIFE.

COVER GALLERY

ED McGUINNESS & CAM SMITH

STUART IMMONEN & JOSÉ MARZÁN, JR.

DOUG MAHNKE & TOM NGUYEN

COVERS

GERMAN GARCIA & JOHN DELL

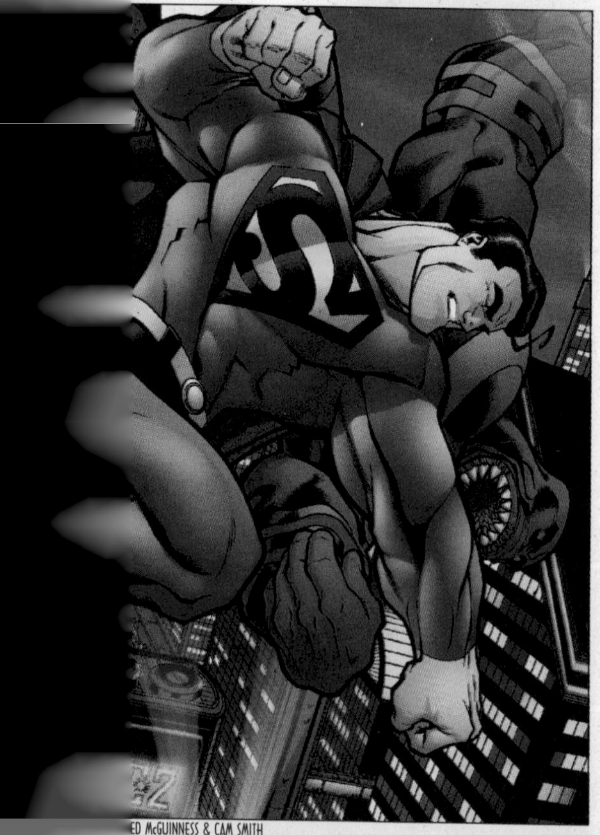

ED McGUINNESS & CAM SMITH

TERRY DODSON & MARK FARMER

SUPERMAN

THE NEVER-ENDING BATTLE CONTINUES IN THESE BOOKS FROM DC COMICS:

FOR READERS OF ALL AGES

SUPERMAN: ADVENTURES OF THE MAN OF STEEL
P. Dini/S. McCloud/R. Burchett/B. Blevins

SUPERMAN: PEACE ON EARTH
Paul Dini/Alex Ross

BATMAN & SUPERMAN ADVENTURES: WORLD'S FINEST
Paul Dini/Joe Staton/Terry Beatty

GRAPHIC NOVELS

SON OF SUPERMAN
H. Chaykin/D. Tischman/J.H. Williams III/M. Gray

SUPERMAN: END OF THE CENTURY
Stuart Immonen/José Marzan Jr.

COLLECTIONS

THE KENTS
J. Ostrander/T. Truman/T. Mandrake/M. Bair

THE DEATH OF SUPERMAN Trilogy
THE DEATH OF SUPERMAN
WORLD WITHOUT A SUPERMAN
THE RETURN OF SUPERMAN
Various writers and artists

SUPERMAN: THE MAN OF STEEL
John Byrne/Dick Giordano

SUPERMAN/DOOMSDAY: HUNTER/PREY
Dan Jurgens/Brett Breeding

SUPERMAN: THE DARK SIDE
J.F. Moore/Kieron Dwyer/Hilary Barta

SUPERMAN: THE DEATH OF CLARK KENT
Various writers and artists

SUPERMAN: THE DOOMSDAY WARS
Dan Jurgens/Norm Rapmund

SUPERMAN: EXILE
Various writers and artists

SUPERMAN FOR ALL SEASONS
Jeph Loeb/Tim Sale

SUPERMAN: KRISIS OF THE KRIMSON KRYPTONITE
Various writers and artists

SUPERMAN: PANIC IN THE SKY
Various writers and artists

SUPERMAN TRANSFORMED!
Various writers and artists

SUPERMAN: THE TRIAL OF SUPERMAN
Various writers and artists

SUPERMAN: THE WEDDING AND BEYOND
Various writers and artists

SUPERMAN: THEY SAVED LUTHOR'S BRAIN
R. Stern/J. Byrne/B. McLeod/J. Guice/K. Dwyer/various

SUPERMAN VS. THE REVENGE SQUAD
Various writers and artists

SUPERMAN: WHATEVER HAPPENED TO THE MAN OF TOMORROW?
A. Moore/C. Swan/G. Pérez/K. Schaffenberger

SUPERMAN: THE DAILIES
Jerry Siegel/Joe Shuster

SUPERMAN: THE SUNDAY CLASSICS
Jerry Siegel/Joe Shuster

SUPERMAN IN THE SIXTIES
Various writers and artists

THE GREATEST SUPERMAN STORIES EVER TOLD
Various writers and artists

LOIS & CLARK: THE NEW ADVENTURES OF SUPERMAN
Various writers and artists

STEEL: THE FORGING OF A HERO
Various writers and artists

SUPERGIRL
P. David/G. Frank/T. Dodson/C. Smith/K. Story

KINGDOM COME
Mark Waid/Alex Ross

LEGENDS OF THE WORLD'S FINEST
Walter Simonson/Dan Brereton

SUPERMAN/BATMAN: ALTERNATE HISTORIES
Various writers and artists

ARCHIVE EDITIONS

SUPERMAN ARCHIVES Vol. 1
(SUPERMAN 1-4)
SUPERMAN ARCHIVES Vol. 2
(SUPERMAN 5-8)
SUPERMAN ARCHIVES Vol. 3
(SUPERMAN 9-12)
SUPERMAN ARCHIVES Vol. 4
(SUPERMAN 13-16)
All by Jerry Siegel/Joe Shuster

SUPERMAN: THE ACTION COMICS ARCHIVES Vol. 1
(ACTION COMICS 1, 7-20)
SUPERMAN: THE ACTION COMICS ARCHIVES Vol. 2
(ACTION COMICS 21-36)
All by Jerry Siegel/Joe Shuster

WORLD'S FINEST COMICS ARCHIVES Vol. 1
(SUPERMAN 76, WORLD'S FINEST 71-85)
B. Finger/E. Hamilton/C. Swan/various

COVERS

DOUG MAHNKE & TOM NGUYEN

YVEL GUICHET & DANNY MIKI

ED McGUINNESS & CAM SMITH